DARE EAT THAT

DARE EAT THAT

DIVYA ANAND

DARE
EAT
THAT

A GUIDE TO BIZARRE FOODS
FROM AROUND THE WORLD

EBURY
PRESS

An imprint of Penguin Random House

EBURY PRESS

USA | Canada | UK | Ireland | Australia
New Zealand | India | South Africa | China | Singapore

Ebury Press is part of the Penguin Random House group of companies
whose addresses can be found at global.penguinrandomhouse.com

Published by Penguin Random House India Pvt. Ltd
4th Floor, Capital Tower 1, MG Road,
Gurugram 122 002, Haryana, India

First published in Ebury Press by Penguin Random House India 2019

Copyright © Divya Anand 2019

ISBN 9780143444664

Typeset in Bembo Std by Manipal Digital Systems, Manipal

Printed at Repro India Limited

To Appa, my first travel companion
and
to Vivek, my forever travel companion

It's a magical world, Hobbes,
ol' buddy . . . Let's go exploring!

—Bill Watterson

Contents

INTRODUCTION

The Origin of the Species

I watched Vivek gasp as he clutched his throat.

'I feel weird,' he choked out as a million thoughts began racing through my head.

I knew puffer fish was poisonous, but one didn't die of puffer fish poisoning if one ate at a licensed restaurant, did they?

This was supposed to be a new milestone in my husband Vivek's quest to eat his way through the world, not the end of it!

How did we even get to this point?

~

I've always been a traveller thanks to my father, who inculcated the love of travel in me by showing me the terracotta warriors at Xian, the ruins of Pompeii and the majestic Angkor Wat temple in Siem Reap before I was a teenager. My way of travelling was to absorb the sights and sounds of the place. Food was never the priority when we travelled—my mother carried her trusty rice-cooker wherever we went and our first stop was always the local supermarket so we could get some curd to make *thayir saadam*,* the go-to comfort food for all

---

* Tamil for curd rice

Tamilians. As long as I got my meals at the right time, I didn't really have a point of view on food.

That is, until, I met my husband, Vivek.

It's almost prophetic that our first meeting was at the cafeteria on the second floor of Hindustan Times House where we both worked. I was eating lunch with a mutual friend and he ambled over to join us, most likely after having haggled extensively with the canteen *wallah* for the best leg piece in the biryani he was eating.

Over the next few months, I got to know Vivek better. He was a true-blue foodie and would go to great lengths to find new food experiences. On weekends or after work, he could be found venturing into the *gullies* of Delhi University for the legendary *chole bhature* or egg rolls. Once, I caught him walking away from the octopus salad at a lunch buffet with an entire reconstructed octopus on his plate. All that remained for everyone else was a pile of limp lettuce leaves. Another time, he convinced a group of co-workers to accompany him on a hunt for chicken-liver fry, something he had frequently eaten in the dhabas of Kanpur. At lunch, one could always trust Vivek to finish off his food and everyone else's!

I was intrigued by his willingness to experiment with something new, irrespective of how bizarre it seemed. It was mind-boggling to a vegetarian, non-foodie like me. Through our conversations, I discovered that it all started with the first bite of pork in the beautiful town of Darjeeling, where he was on a vacation with his college classmates. For someone who had only eaten chicken and some local varieties of fish in his hometown of Gorakhpur, breaking through the mental barrier of eating pork was a very big deal. His family and friends were clear about what constituted as 'meat' and pig wasn't a part of their definition. However, in Darjeeling, he saw pork being sold and eaten as commonly as if it were chicken and not as something that was unacceptable. He grabbed a piece off his friend's plate and consumed his first bite of forbidden food. Once he got past this mental barrier, he realized that one could potentially eat anything—all the 'rules' were fungible based on places and cultures.

After this, the inherent foodie in Vivek took over and he began looking for new cuisines, tastes and things he hadn't tried before everywhere he went. Every city had something different to offer—in Varanasi, he enjoyed the sweets and *lassi*; in Lucknow the *ulta tawa parantha* and mutton *galouti kabab*; in Delhi, he scavenged the by-lanes of Chandni Chowk and Purani Dilli; and in Pune, he was introduced to Malvani and Kolhapuri cuisines.

Pune is also where Vivek met and befriended a group of his colleagues who were also open to experimenting with food. For the first time, he had like-minded friends with whom he could explore Pune and nearby areas, dish by dish. Together, they found and ate exotic species like quail, emu and rabbits. It was around this time that we started dating, even though we no longer lived in the same city. I would hear all about their exploits on a regular basis.

One day, he sent me an email with no subject line and just an image attached. I opened it expecting to see the latest dish he'd eaten during one of his food treks. Instead, I saw a chart that reminded me of the 'animal kingdom' chart from my science textbooks at school. On one side, there were invertebrates classified into molluscs, crustaceans and other complicated biological classifications. On the other side, the vertebrates were broken into Pisces and mammals. Under each of these classifications, there were photos of animals, fish and other sea creatures with labels to call out what they were.

'What is this chart you sent me,' I asked him, when we spoke later in the day.

'That's my progress chart. It's what I've eaten so far,' he said.

At that moment, I realized Vivek's love for food had now reached a level of professionalism and I was stuck with a food adventurer for life. Luckily for him, I was an explorer at heart and loved the adventure involved in tracking down a new species that could be eaten, even if I wasn't to eat it myself.

While Vivek was busy cataloguing his exploits, I moved to Berkeley, California to pursue a second master's degree. Suddenly, I was plunged into a world that traversed cultures from around the globe. I quickly realized that the best way for me to explore the multitude of cultures surrounding me was through the food. As I took trips through the US to Chicago, New York and the Midwest, I moved past sticking to the foods I was comfortable with and began exploring all the cuisines that the country offered: from hand-rolled noodles at a hole-in-the-wall Chinese restaurant, to sharing a giant dinner plate at an Ethiopian restaurant, to the best ramen in Hell's Kitchen. While I was now open to trying chicken or seafood in order to experience a cuisine, I was still most comfortable with eating the vegetarian options where they existed. Even with Vivek's influence, I never gathered the courage to eat bizarre species—not then and not now, after four years of watching Vivek's experiments live. I was able to bring myself out of my comfort zone to this point, but haven't managed to get any further.

In the winter of 2014, we got married. The wedding began at one end of the country and ended at the other. The *baraat* that started on the Chennai Express train from

Gorakhpur culminated in three wedding receptions, the last of which was in Coimbatore. After fourteen days of wedding festivities and travelling across the country for the various functions, we headed on our first trip together to the Maldives. By now, the chart was beginning to branch out to species that went beyond what you'd expect to see in a standard restaurant menu.

In Seattle, where Vivek and I spent a few months right after our wedding, he was able to explore the city and its food more intimately than I'd managed in the year I'd lived there. Every day, he would tell me about a new street, a new supermarket and a new restaurant. When I asked my co-workers about them, I realized he'd found corners of the city that even long-time Seattleites didn't know of!

As he combined his explorations with new dishes, I quickly realized that his quest to eat every species could be combined with my lifelong dream to travel the world. Over the next three years, we travelled to the UK, Sri Lanka, Thailand, Luxembourg, France, Australia, Cambodia, Tanzania and Vietnam. Our travels were filled with adventure. For Vivek, the adventure was in eating something new and bizarre. For me, the adventure was in being able to find something new and elusive—it was like a detective game to research, track and find the next species for Vivek to eat. The thrill of the chase was far more interesting to me than the actual dish itself and so, I left the eating of the bizarre species to Vivek. This quest helped me explore better, to see places I would not have seen otherwise—wet markets, street food markets and insect farms began featuring on our itineraries. We became better at playing dumb charades with the locals in every country. I soon realized that food is the one thing that cuts across language, culture and borders to connect people. With every new species that Vivek ate, I found a new place, a new experience and a new story to tell.

This book is a catalogue of our best food adventures and a guide for bizarre foods in each of these countries. We've used diary entries to capture the sights, sounds and smells of the place and to catalogue what species we found, the price and how they taste. We hope to share what we've learned through our travels—the new things we've learned as well as some of the unexpected twists we experienced.

If you have an interest in seeing the world through the lens of culinary anthropology, these rules should be your starting point:

Open yourself to new experiences: Different foods have different meanings across cultures and there's no reason why you should eat one thing and not the other. This is easier said than done, which I completely understand given that I haven't found the courage to eat bizarre foods as Vivek has. I empathize with his drive but haven't completely broken down my own mental boundaries.

Food tastes better at the source: The closer you are to the origin of a food, the better it will taste. For us, trying to find food at the source has resulted in some hilarious not-so-successful attempts at fishing, and visits to all kinds of farms, including a cricket farm!

Shop local, eat local: Visiting the local markets allowed us to find the best versions of the local food.

All good things are found in Chinatown: Chinatown is a mini-China that never fails to surprise and yield new species for one to eat. Until we manage our still-elusive trip to China, Chinatown is the best substitute for finding new delicacies.

Serendipity is the key ingredient to finding weird food: While we go looking for weird food, there are times when the food seems to find us. It helps that our travel styles are so different—I like to plan and Vivek likes to go in whichever direction looks interesting. The combination often results in some serendipitous findings.

Eat futuristically: Scientists, the world over, have researched solutions to the world food crisis and converge upon eating insects and seaweed as the solution.[1] We've travelled through many parts of Southeast Asia to understand how sustainable these options are and why many cultures have always eaten them so we're prepared for the apocalypse.

These guidelines have helped on our journey of adventurous eating. While the quest to eat every species is ongoing, we hope that our experiences help you eat your way through a country as a means to explore the local culture!

How to Read the Rating Chart

All the food in this book has been rated by 'Taste' and 'Fear Factor'.

The tastes are rated on a scale from 1–5 where 1 is insipid and 5 is a dance of the taste buds. 'Fear Factor' is rated on a scale from 1–5 where 1 is something that anyone can eat and 5 is something that even Vivek was afraid to eat until he dared to eat it.

Taste

★	Insipid
★★	Edible
★★★	Palatable
★★★★	Delicious
★★★★★	Dance of the taste buds

Fear Factor

1	Anyone can eat that
2	Try to eat that
3	Proceed with caution
4	Don't try this at home
5	Dare eat that!

**UNITED
STATES**

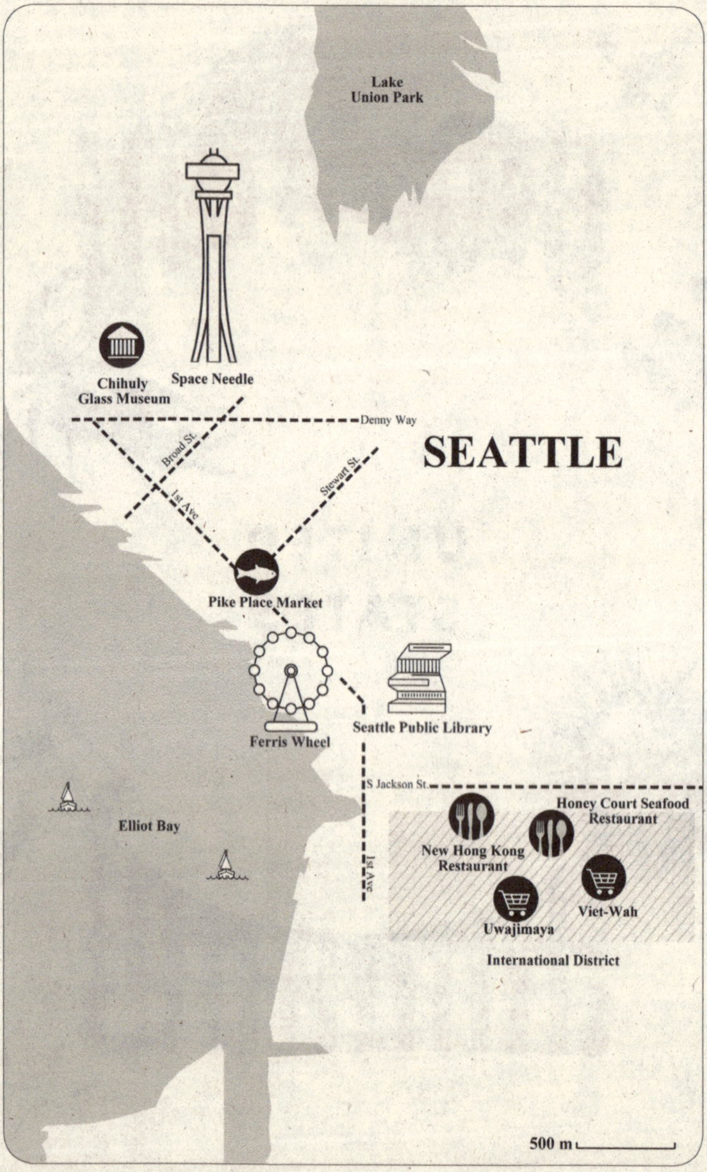

Lake
Union Park

Chihuly
Glass Museum

Space Needle

Denny Way

Broad St.

1st Ave.

Stewart St.

SEATTLE

Pike Place Market

Ferris Wheel

Seattle Public Library

S Jackson St.

1st Ave.

Elliot Bay

Honey Court Seafood
Restaurant

New Hong Kong
Restaurant

Uwajimaya

Viet-Wah

International District

500 m

The United States of America is a medley of cultures that come together to create a vibrant country. It's home to beautiful beaches, snow-covered mountains, art museums, historical monuments and more. From the glittery extravagance of Vegas, to the shining lights of LA, to fast-paced New York and laidback Hawaii, the US has something for every traveller. Lovers of natural beauty cannot go wrong irrespective of whether they choose to lose themselves in the hillsides of the Great Plains, stare into the vast abyss of the Grand Canyon, trek through the lush rainforests of the Pacific Northwest, or wander around the scenic country lanes of New England. In fact, to truly experience the multiplicity at the soul of the US, most people would recommend living there. If not, a solid vacation would still require about 3–4 weeks to just about see the top spots on one coast.

For us, the US was home, albeit for a very short time. I was living in Seattle when we were first married and Vivek visited me to experience living in the US. It gave Vivek his first experience with world food. He discovered Vietnamese frogs' legs at Ba Bar, a restaurant in Seattle's Capitol Hill. This was followed by many days of exploring and finding freeze-dried insects and other exotic species in Chinatown, followed by being able to witness the world's largest fishing auction in Hawaii. These experiences helped him add new classes like insects to the food chart that tracked every species he ate. As the food chart grew, he realized that he could become a modern-day Phileas Fogg, the protagonist in Jules Verne's novel *Around the World in Eighty Days*, who ate his way around the globe.[2]

Our food explorations in the US thus mark the beginning of our journey to travel the world and learn about every culture through its food.

One Fish, Two Fish, Red Fish, Blue Fish

Pike Place Market is one of the oldest continuously operated farmers' markets in the United States. The market overlooks Seattle's Elliot Bay waterfront and is the place of business for many farmers, business owners and craftspeople. The market is on a steep hill and has five levels. The main atrium is riddled with farmers' markets and fishmongers selling fresh produce, making it a riot of colours and smells. The atrium also houses multiple restaurants including Seattle icons like 'Piroshki Piroshki' (*piroshky* is a Russian puff pastry, made of baked or fried buns stuffed with a variety of fillings), the original Starbucks, The Crumpet Shop and Ellenos Greek Yogurt. The open area of the market, just beyond the atrium, is filled with quirky craftsmen selling everything from painted glass bottles to jewellery to watercolour magnets. The lower floors are filled with every type of store one could ever imagine— antique stores, magic shops, comic book collectibles and even one of the oldest head shops* in Seattle!

I lived in Seattle from the summer of 2014 to the fall of 2015. In the year that I was a Seattle local, I had many friends and family visit me. In the process of showing them around

---

* An outlet specializing in cannabis and tobacco paraphernalia

town, I came up with my own version of a day tour across downtown Seattle. I would start by taking people up on the Seattle Great Wheel, the Ferris Wheel by the waterfront. On a clear day, the Wheel offers great aerial views of the pier and the city skyline. From here, we would walk to the Pike Place Market. I also added other local attractions to this list based on peoples' interests. For the history buffs, we would take the cruise around Elliot Bay, featuring an audio history of Seattle and a visit to the Boeing Museum; for music lovers, a trip to the Experience Music Project Museum (renamed MoPoP Museum in 2016) which showcases the best in pop culture; for the art aficionados, a visit to the Chihuly Glass Museum, my personal favourite and home to some spectacular glass sculptures.

On Vivek's first weekend in Seattle, we went to the Ferris Wheel, followed by a walk through the market. Despite it being the middle of winter, it was a clear day and we got a great view of the central business district and the boats out on the bay from the top of the Ferris Wheel. I took us to the market through Post Alley, a street that houses the infamous Gum Wall, a wall covered by chewed up bubble gum. The Wall is by the box office for the Market Theatre. In 1993, the patrons of Unexpected Productions Seattle Theatresports unwittingly started the tradition of sticking gum on the wall by doing this before a performance.[3] Theatre workers worked hard to get rid of the gum, but eventually gave up. I did not give Vivek any precursor to the Wall in order to see his reaction when he visited what is one of the top five germiest tourist attractions in the world. Contrary to my expectations, he remained unfazed. Clearly, someone who is open to eating some of the most bizarre foods in the world has a high tolerance for weird things!

Vivek is a huge comic book buff, so I took him towards the lower levels of the market where I knew there was a quirky comic book collectibles store that he would love. However, the maze that is Pike Place proved to be too much for me. I'm so directionally challenged that I sometimes have trouble finding my table after visiting the restroom at a restaurant! We wandered around in circles in an attempt to find the little alley that the store was located in. Unlike the last time I was in the market, there wasn't anybody in a Darth Vader costume standing outside the alley to guide us into the shop. Somehow, in the process of looking for the elusive Darth Vader, we ended up walking back up onto the main level.

We found ourselves right under the 'Public Market Center' sign at the corner of Pike Place, the actual entrance to the market. We were right next to 'Rachel the Pig'—a bronze cast piggy bank that weighs 250 kg, made by local artist Georgia Gerber and modelled after a real pig, also called Rachel, that won a county fair. Legend has it that if you rub her snout and make a donation, you will have good luck. Rachel earns around $6000–9000 a year in various currencies, which is used to fund the market's social services. I suggested we add to her earnings in return for some good luck, hoping that would lead us to the collectibles store. But Vivek was sceptical.

'A dollar for good luck!' he exclaimed. 'I wouldn't ever put that much in a *daan peti** in India!'

He believed it was too much to donate to a giant piggy bank. Eventually, he found an errant one rupee coin and decided it was okay to donate in Indian rupees.

'After all, pigs don't understand currencies,' he declared, as he rubbed Rachel's snout.

---

* Hindi word for donation box

Despite my asking, he wouldn't tell me what he wished for. Now, after four years of travelling with him, I believe he asked her for luck on his quest to eat as many new species as possible. That would explain his unerring luck with locating new foods even when he isn't looking for them.

The crowds waiting to rub Rachel's snout pale in comparison to the crowds wandering the arcade behind her. The arcade is filled with produce stalls, meat stalls and craftspeople. On one end of this arcade is a line of produce and flower stalls selling fresh fruit, vegetables and bouquets. On the other end, directly behind Rachel, is the Pike Place Fish Company, a fishmonger that became famous after it was featured in the book, *Fish! A Remarkable Way to Boost Morale and Improve Results!* Even if it hadn't featured in the book, it would still be remembered vividly by anyone who visits the market.

The employees wear bright orange uniforms that ensure you can spot them from anywhere in the arcade. There are two sections to the stall—an ice-covered table that displays the catch of the day and other items and the area behind the counter where the fish are prepped for sale. When a customer points to a fish, an employee stationed near the fish at the ice-covered fish table will pick it up and hurl it over the countertop where another employee will catch the fish and prepare it. The employees sing through the process of throwing, catching and prepping the fish. This mini performance is a very well-synced routine and one can never tire of watching it.

Local lore has it that this tradition began when fishmongers got tired of having to walk to the fish table to retrieve salmon every time a customer ordered one. Eventually, the owner realized it was easier to station an employee at the table to throw the fish over the counter. There's no backstory for why the singing began.

We waited by the stall to watch the performance. While we waited for someone to buy a fish, Vivek began examining the display. He was excited to see all the different varieties of fish they stocked. He made notes on his phone every time he came across something interesting. I started reading the signs, which had one-liners written on them, like the one that proudly proclaimed, 'We only sell wild fish caught by wild fisherman.' I wondered how wild this fisherman was and whether he'd wrestled the fish out of the sea instead of catching it.

Wild salmon caught by wild fishermen

While I contemplated the wild fisherman's methods, Vivek was busy examining the catch and exclaiming that the name 'Season's Open Fresh Whole Copper River Sockeye Salmon' was the best name he'd ever heard for a food item. He has a general grouse that people are too generic with names and this level of specificity is what he had been looking for in every display and menu. He continued to make notes on his phone of all the species he saw—Large Pacific Oysters, Rock Lobsters and Jumbo Alaskan King. When I asked him what the list was for, he told me that he was noting down species so he could look them up later to learn more. He also wanted to see if these were unique to this area or if he'd already eaten them because there is often more than one given name for a species. Watching him made me realize how he seemed to know so much more about animals than I did. I am no longer surprised when he spouts animal trivia that even a safari guide is unaware of because I know it is a result of years of extensive food research!

Pike Place fishing—the Fish Company

As we looked through their wares, we spotted a row of transparent takeaway glasses submerged on snow-like ice. The sign said these were shrimp cocktails. Each glass had a large pink and white shrimp placed around the rim, as though the shrimp were trying to climb out of the glass. Each shrimp had a lemon wedge placed on top of it, like a rakish hat for the escaping shrimp. Vivek pounced on the shrimp as it was his chance to eat something right away. There was no place to sit so he relished his shrimp cocktail as he stood by the display and continued to greedily glance at the other goodies. Up close, the shrimp was bright and shiny red, with fresh meat glistening through the cracks in the skin. It reminded me of the fruit *chaat* in Delhi. No wonder Bubba, from Forrest Gump,[4] said that shrimp is the fruit of the sea! The shrimp was sweet and succulent, a sucker punch of flavours.

As he ate, another customer bought a fish. This was the moment we'd been waiting for! Immediately, the salesperson at the front of the shop threw it across to the cashier as the others began to sing their synchronized ditty. The salesperson in the front even added a few dance steps to his performance that day. At the other end, the employees of the Pike Place Fish Co. attempted to convince a buyer to throw them the fish and join their performance. He didn't give in. Vivek, however, loved that part and said he would've wanted to also 'catch' his order if he were the one buying and participating in the performance. We rounded off his Pike Place experience by grabbing a coffee from one of Seattle's other famous landmarks—the first ever Starbucks outlet.

We didn't end up finding the comic book store we went looking for that morning but we were able to stumble upon a different experience. I always plan my itineraries until the last minute. This is diametrically opposite to how Vivek travels; he prefers a more laidback, 'wander till you find what you want' style. Getting lost in Pike Place Market meant that I got a taste of his version of travelling. Our walk through Pike Place was one of those times when the travel was more about the journey than about the destination.

The Pike Place Fish Company, Pike Place Market, 85 Pike Street	
Item	*Shrimp Cocktail*
Taste	★★★★
Price	$4
Fear Factor	2
New Species	None

To Eat a Mocking Bird

When we spot a street that has an arched gateway with dragon heads on either end, we know we are at Chinatown. Irrespective of which country we are in, entering Chinatown always feels like stepping into a mini-China. Inside Chinatown, all the stores and restaurants have distinctly Chinese artwork, signs and decor. After dark, the streets are a riot of colour. Bright red and yellow lanterns illuminate every doorway, welcoming you to eat Chinese food or shop for Chinese trinkets. Chinatown is always a great stop for the food and the ambience.

The very first time Vivek visited a Chinatown was in Seattle. He was wandering around the Asian markets in the hope of finding something interesting to eat when he stumbled upon it. His very first discovery was the jellyfish at the New Hong Kong Restaurant.

A plate arrived with what looked like wrinkly noodles and Vivek poked around trying to find the pieces of jellyfish. After a few minutes, he took a bite of the noodles. He soon realized that these weren't noodles, but shredded bits of jellyfish. The main taste of the dish came from the spicy sauce, a mix of soy sauce and sesame oil, which was balanced by the chilling effect of the cold salad. But the true experience came from the texture—jellyfish, as the name suggests, is a lot like Jell-O. It has no form or shape and is extremely chewy in texture. The success of the jellyfish experiment inspired Vivek to set out on more Chinatown adventures.

Jellyfish cold plate—jellyfish never die, they get eaten

Later that evening, once he was home, he said, 'Did you know that jellyfish never die?'

'Ew! You ate a living thing! That's disgusting!' I exclaimed.

'No, that's not what I said,' he said shaking his head. 'Jellyfish don't age, so they can't die of old age. They live forever until some other fish eats them. Or, well, *someone*. Today that someone was me!'

New Hong Kong Restaurant, 900 South Jackson Street	
Item	*Jellyfish Cold Plate*
Taste	★★★
Price	$15
Fear Factor	4
New Species	Jellyfish

~

On his walks through Chinatown, Vivek wandered into restaurants, grocery stores, fresh produce stores, medicine shops—pretty much any of the stores that looked like they carried items he couldn't identify. He would then interview sales reps about all the unidentifiable items. He came across a variety of things of interest, not all of which were ready to eat. The fresh produce shops carried frogs, rabbits, abalone, sea cucumber, clams, oysters, pig blood pouches and silkworms alongside regulars like happy-looking pig heads and decapitated duck heads sold in transparent packets.

During every one of these trips, he thanked the meat packagers wise enough to put the photo of the animal on the package. Packagers often purposefully do not put images of the animals on the face of the packets as they don't want consumers to associate the food with the picture. This is something the food industry calls a 'best practice'. This is in spite of the fact that this puts consumers like Vivek, who do not speak the language of the countries where these foods originate, in a tough situation. He would see a package and his instinct would tell him this was something new. But the lack of English descriptions meant that he couldn't figure out what it actually was and know, for certain, whether this was a new food. This, coupled with the fact that most salespeople didn't speak English, made the situation difficult. Most people come into stores wanting to eat what they know. Vivek, on the other hand, was walking into stores wanting to eat what he couldn't identify!

During a visit to the Viet Wah Supermarket, he discovered a package of top snails cooked in coconut milk. The packaging was in English and claimed this was 'Sunrise Wild Caught Cooked Top Snail with Coconut Juice'. To make matters easier, it featured a photo of lots of snails in a plate. It also said, 'Ready to Cook. Microwavable Container.' The rest was in a different language, but he felt this was sufficient information and purchased it.

Top snails are marine snails that have shells in the shape of a top, approximately the size of a thumb. Since the snail lives inside the shell, there's a small amount of meat within the shell.

Ready to eat top snails

To eat it, one needs to either pull out the meat with a safety pin or suck on the shell as if it were a straw to dislodge the meat. It was a major task to finish half a kilogram of the tiny snails but he enjoyed the fruits of his labour. Snails, like most other shellfish, have a silky earthiness that mimics the taste of the ocean. It was like eating a bean that came out of a tough pod. These snails also had a creamy texture from the coconut juice which resulted in something that tasted like the savoury version of salted caramel ice cream.

Viet Wah Supermarket, 1032 S Jackson Street	
Item	*Top Snails*
Taste	★★★
Price	$10
Fear Factor	4
New Species	Snails

~

On Vivek's next trip to Chinatown, he stumbled upon an interesting restaurant. The receptionist got him a table, but couldn't converse with him beyond that. He soon realized this wasn't specific to the receptionist—no one there could speak English. He wondered how he would manage to find any of the new species that were hidden in the menu. He was thrilled to discover they had an English menu. He scanned it and nearly dropped it in excitement. They were serving fried squab!

Squab is a young domestic pigeon raised for the express purpose of consumption. These pigeons are picked when they've grown enough to provide meat for consumption before they start flying. This timing ensures that the meat isn't too tough as flying toughens the muscles.

He was about to place an order when he realized that servers were passing by with carts, ready to serve him various varieties of dim sum from the bamboo baskets stacked on the cart. The carts were serving people in a manner similar to the *thaali* system in an Indian restaurant. No one seemed to be ordering anything in particular and no one seemed to be taking orders either. Any conversation he overheard sounded like it was happening in Mandarin. He was worried that he was going to attempt to place an a la carte order at a buffet-only restaurant.

As he was wondering what to do, a server came up to him. She stopped and opened up one of the bamboo baskets. He shook his head to indicate that he didn't want it. She tried again with some other options and he kept refusing them all. She looked a little surprised, or so he imagined, that he was refusing lunch. He then pointed out the item he wanted on the menu. She smiled and nodded at him and then headed towards the kitchen.

He hoped she had understood him. In any case, if the confusion resulted in a dish weirder than squab, it would become his appetizer, and the squab, his entrée. After all, he reasoned, one must not look a gift horse in the mouth, especially in Chinatown where gift horses abound. While he waited, he wondered if he'd even know if he was served some other bird. Ultimately, all birds have the same body parts and look similar when served. The server interrupted his inner monologue as she walked up with a plate unlike any Vivek had seen before. It was unmistakably a pigeon.

A pigeon complete with a head, eyes and beak, perched upright on the plate, much like how live pigeons perch on a balcony grill. He stared at this golden-brown fried pigeon that appeared to be looking right at him. Vivek has never been squeamish about food, but even he was slightly uncomfortable while looking back at this bird. In order to assuage his guilt, he decided to have a quick conversation with it before he ate it. Maybe he was bored sitting by himself or maybe the bird was so life-like he felt the need to introduce himself before he took his first bite.

'*Aur? Sab theek?*'* he asked the pigeon, almost as if it were an old friend from Gorakhpur.

---

* All well?

'I hope you didn't have too much trouble getting here. Are you from the US or an immigrant,' he inquired.

The bird didn't dignify this question with a response.

'*Waise ek baat bataiye*,' he said, lapsing back into Hindi as the bird was behaving like an old friend who was miffed with him. '*Aapki chamakti hui twacha ka raaz kya hai? Almond oil ya refined oil? Pet main ek murgi hai, usko aap yeh raaz zaroor bataiye.*'*

He then proceeded to laugh at his own joke, looking expectantly at the bird to join in. There was nary a squawk in response, proving that it was well and truly cooked.

He began eating it slowly and systematically, all the while humming '*Kabootar kha, kha, kha*'† to the tune of '*Kabootar ja, ja, ja*'‡ as if he were singing *to* his supper.

Despite the oddity of presentation, the pigeon was more flavourful and tender than any other bird he had eaten. It had a strong taste since the bird had been cooked with the skin. The skin was thicker and fatter than chicken skin and was crisp from the roasting. The meat was also darker and juicier than chicken.

He immediately let me know that he had eaten a member of the pigeon family. I was thrilled. I have hated pigeons after a horrifying pigeon-related incident in the year 2007. A pigeon flew into my hostel room at SPJIMR in Mumbai, where I was doing my MBA. My roommate and I were away on our two–month long autumn internship project and had left the

---

* So, tell me, what's the secret behind your glowing skin? Is it almond oil or refined oil? There's a chicken in my stomach, tell it your secrets when you meet.
† Eat, eat, eat the pigeon
‡ Fly, fly, fly away, pigeon

windows open by accident. The pigeon, which hadn't spotted us for a while, took our absence as a sign that we weren't ever coming back and proceeded to relieve itself over all our stuff. We returned to a room that reeked and had to spend a lot of our hard-earned internship stipend towards disinfecting the room. Since then, I have carried a one-woman vendetta against the species.

On that day, I felt vindicated. That Mumbai pigeon and I were finally even.

Honey Court Seafood Restaurant, 516 Maynard Ave S	
Item	*Roasted Squab*
Taste	★★★★
Price	$11
Fear Factor	5
New Species	Squab

The Duck and the Egg

'D, you will not believe what I found today!' said Vivek enthusiastically, when I got home from work one evening. He had been visiting Chinatown a lot while I was at work, so I had asked him to look for Wasabi Kit Kat. I had heard that it was one of the special flavours available only in Japan and, since I didn't know anyone visiting Japan soon, I wanted Vivek to see if he could locate it on his explorations.

'Did you find the Wasabi Kit Kat?' I asked hopefully.

'No, I didn't. I got some Matcha Kit Kat, though,' he said. 'But that isn't important. I found something MUCH better in a small Vietnamese grocery store in the Uwajimaya neighbourhood while walking back home. I found *balut!*'

Something about his expression told me I would regret asking questions. I was okay not knowing details about some of Vivek's finds, especially those of the Chinatown variety. Up until this point, his explorations had stayed outside the house, but now it sounded like he had brought something home. Before I could decide how I felt about having something bizarre in my kitchen, he pulled out an egg tray from the fridge. These eggs looked like a bigger version of standard table eggs, so I couldn't really understand what all the fuss was about.

'Um, you bought eggs? But we just bought a tray of eggs yesterday,' I said.

'These are not just any eggs,' he said huffily. 'Balut is a delicacy in Philippines and Vietnam. I cannot believe I found these in Seattle. The storekeeper only had a pack of one dozen, so I bought it. Anyway, I'm going to boil these for dinner, so don't make anything for me.'

I didn't want any more details about this balut, whatever it was, as long as I didn't have to cook. I pulled out my book and went back to reading. Vivek started looking for ways to cook balut. A few minutes later, he went to the fridge, took out his precious tray of the eggs and started discussing cooking methods with me.

'The guy at the store said these are to be boiled before eating, but many Filipinos recommend eating them raw to truly experience the flavour. What do you think?' he asked.

'Do what you want. Raw eggs are gross, so you may want to boil them. About ten minutes is the norm with regular eggs, so it should be good for these,' I said.

'Okay. But do you think ten minutes of boiling is enough for the head?'

That got my attention.

'The head? What head?' I asked.

'You know that balut is a half-formed duck? It's a 15–20 day old . . .'

'WHAT! Boil it! Boil it well so you don't get staph infection!' I screeched at a decibel level that could have cracked those eggs open right then.

I should have talked him out of the whole experiment. I should have convinced him to return the eggs for a refund or raise twelve ducks as his own in our tiny apartment. But when I saw how eager he was about eating balut, I couldn't ask him to do either. I compromised by asking him to boil them for a good half-hour.

Balut—Is it a bird, an egg, or something else?

Then, I shot a video of him eating it. That video is a true testament to love.* Imagine watching someone eat an egg where you can see the semi-formed features! Balut is incubated for 14–21 days before it is boiled and eaten. Forget building monuments to commemorate your love. In today's day and age, I recommend that all couples test their relationship with the balut method.

I could see the veins popping out of the top of the head as he ate it. There was a black spot-like thing on one side that might have been an eye, but I'd rather not think about that. Vivek has eaten many bizarre foods before and after balut, but this tops my list of the most bizarre foods I've seen him eat.

Balut is also very filling. It's a very rich and thick egg, more so than the eggs we are used to. The whites were a

---

* For more photos and videos of balut and other bizarre foods, log on to www.dareeatthat.com

tougher and more rubbery version of (regular) egg whites and
the yellows were like dry egg yolks. The veins and vaguely
formed body parts were strong in taste and Vivek claimed it
tasted like half-bird, half-egg.

Despite his assurances that he would finish all twelve eggs
in a single sitting, he couldn't eat more than two at a time.
Eventually, he had to throw away half the tray.

'I'm worried that I will soon have ducklings following me
around thinking I'm their mother,' he said as he threw away
the rest of the tray.

Grocery Store, International District	
Item	*Boiled Balut*
Taste	★★★
Price	$1 per balut
Fear Factor	5
New Species	Balut

Recipe: Balut

Ingredients
1 tray of balut eggs
A handful of Vietnamese laksa leaves
1 lemon
Salt and pepper to taste
Spades of willpower
Friend/significant other to catalogue the process

Method
Start with 2 or 3 balut eggs. If you're able to consume those,
    you can use the rest of your tray.

Boil the eggs for at least half an hour. It's the least you can do if you must eat half formed ducks!

Season with salt and pepper.

Serve eggs with the laksa leaves with a tinge of lemon squeezed over them.

Enjoy!

North Pacific Ocean

O'AHU ISLAND
HAWAII

Pearl Harbor
Museum

Pearl Harbor

Pier 38

HAWAIIAN ISLANDS

5 km

Fresh off the Boat

Hawaii is known for its world-famous beaches spread across eight islands. It's also the site of Pearl Harbor. The Japanese bombing of Pearl Harbor was the cause of the United States entering the Second World War. Today, one can visit Pearl Harbor to see the site, as well as the Arizona Memorial, the USS Bowfin and the Pacific Aviation Museum. My father, a history buff, wanted to soak in all this and insisted that we go on a vacation to Hawaii while he was visiting us.

We were on our way to Oahu with my parents when I discovered that Vivek had a hidden agenda for coming along—he wanted to see the fish market at Honolulu. Oahu is a large island and he was hoping to sample the many kinds of seafood there. Honolulu, in Oahu, is also the only place in the US where one can watch a tuna auction as well as a fresh fish auction of any kind between Tokyo in the East and Maine in the West.

The thought of being able to witness an auction of this scale was enough to convince a night owl like Vivek to wake up at dawn. The uniqueness of the auction convinced me to tag along as well. Our co-travellers, my parents, opted out so they could be well-rested before we went on a whirlwind sightseeing tour of Pearl Harbor. They were still asleep when we left to take the bus to Pier 38 where the auction buildings are located. The bus dropped us off a short walk away from the pier.

The path to the pier had the ocean on one side and the warehouses on the other. We moved closer and saw boats of different sizes, including some fishing boats that looked like they had just come back from a trip at sea. We walked towards the building of the United Fishing Agency where the Honolulu Fish Auction takes place.

Fishermen in Hawaii have access to prized large fish like tuna, mahi-mahi and moonfish, thanks to the access they have to the Pacific Ocean. This drives the local economy. Each tuna fish costs a few thousand dollars and there are some, depending on size and weight, that can cost as much as tens of thousands of dollars. Fishing vessels are unloaded at around 1 a.m. to prepare for the auction. The catch is inspected, weighed, tagged and then displayed on pallets for the auction.

The auctioneers begin the auctioning at 5.30 a.m. We roamed around the warehouses before we located the area where there was a lot of activity. This side of the auction building had low doors where trailers were parked. Fish were unloaded through these doors on big boxes of ice. There was an additional chill in the air, beyond the early morning nip that one would expect at this time. Men with thick boots and waterproof jackets were carrying long metal rods with hooks at one end. They were using these rods to haul the fish over the short distance from the warehouse doors to the back of the trucks. We heard sounds from the auction coming from within the building, so we decided to find a way to get inside.

The fish were being unloaded through the small windows at the ground level, almost like a service entrance for fish. These windows were covered with plastic blinds like the ones found on conveyor belts at the airport. There was a large entrance on one side that also contained several blinds to keep the temperature within low. We weren't sure if someone who wasn't a seller or a buyer could enter the premises. We decided to start out by walking into the administrative office that we spotted on the side, to see if we could find out. On the way, we spotted posters—'Rules for Trading Fish', 'Which Species to Engage With' and so on—which gave us a glimpse into a fisherman's life. There were rewards for fishermen who spotted a catch with an electronic tag on it, indicating that these were species monitored for research. Tagging enables researchers to understand the movement, distribution and abundance of these species in the water. The rewards ranged from $100 for mako and thresher sharks to $500 for albacore tuna. Fishermen were expected to send the fish to the Marine Department with its tag, the latitude and longitude of the location of the catch and the gear with which it was caught to get the reward.[5]

We asked the officer at the desk of the office if we could attend the auction. She said that we couldn't enter the building wearing flip-flops and also informed us that the only way to attend if we weren't buyers, was to come for the official tour on a Saturday morning. Since it wasn't a Saturday morning, I was sure this was the end of our auction experience. Vivek didn't give up as quickly and persuaded her to let us in. She agreed and even lent us some protective boots. The boots were large and almost pant-like in length, going up to our knees. They were also heavy, ensuring that we didn't accidentally injure ourselves with one of the six-foot-long iron hooks that the fishermen were wielding like golf sticks.

At the entrance to the auction area, there was a large tray of disinfectant that we needed to step into before we entered the hall. Entering the hall felt like stepping into a freezer.

Surprisingly, it had no smell at all. I'd expected it to smell like
fish, like the fish markets in India. Here, all that one could
smell was a draught of chilly damp air. It turns out that frozen
fish has no smell.

The hall was large, without any rooms or partitions. Fish
were being transported in on low, flat trolleys through the
windows we'd seen outside. I'd never seen such giant fish
before and was surprised to realize the actual size of tuna. They
were at least a metre wide and laid in long rows along the aisle.
As I gaped at the large muscular fish that looked like they had
been carved from a single piece of wood, Vivek talked about
his plans to visit Japan and eat tuna eyeballs, a delicacy that's
only available there.

I kept looking at the fish and saw that each one had a
sticker pasted on it with a number. Each fish also had a small
wedge-shaped piece of flesh cut out and placed on top of
their bodies. Bidders were examining these wedges much
like we do for watermelons to check their freshness and
quality.

We moved to an aisle where a group of men were
slowly moving from fish to fish. We knew they were likely
to be buyers and eavesdropped in the hopes that we would
understand how they judged the catch. They were talking
to each other in low, serious voices as they moved from
one fish to the next. The auctioneer held a clipboard and
kept mumbling as the group moved forward. His mumbles
sounded like a chant of sorts. Every once in a while, one
or more of the others would break the chant by interjecting
with their own mumbles as they placed their bids. In a few
minutes, the auctioneer would scribble on a sticker book,
peel off the sticker and paste it on the fish to signify the close
of the auction.

Tuna auction: Nothing like a fish market

'I always thought fish auctions would be loud,' Vivek whispered. 'This is as coldly methodical as the air inside the warehouse!'

We spent an hour walking through the auction room with the bidders, trying to observe everything they did. We considered speaking to them to understand the process better, but everyone here was hard at work and their tense faces did not encourage any questioning from gate-crashers like us. After all, they were betting on fish worth thousands of dollars every minute! Bluefin tuna went from being a largely ignored fish to one of the most popular varieties once sushi caught on in the US. Once it became the most sought-after fish, the quantities dwindled, making it rare and expensive. The tuna buyers in that auction were busy bidding on what was likely the world's most expensive fish.

When we got back to our hotel, my parents asked us how the auction was and Vivek began describing it in extreme detail.

'The buyers' facial expressions remained the same throughout—cold, transactional and computational. I felt like I was watching a game while simultaneously trying to understand the rules,' he said. 'I really wanted to bid and bring back a 200-pound fish to the hotel room, if I could. Now I'm craving tuna steak, so I hope you will be okay with making a pit stop at a seafood restaurant,' he added, as he began googling 'biggest seafood restaurant in Honolulu'.

My vegetarian parents were speechless.

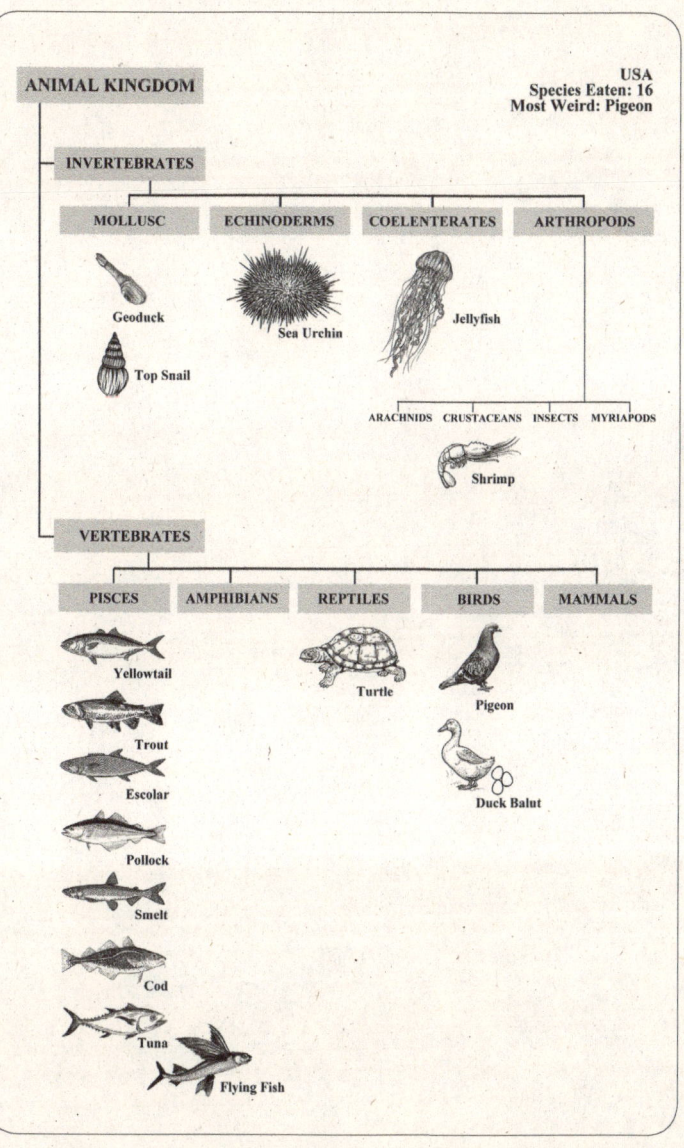

ANIMAL KINGDOM

USA
Species Eaten: 16
Most Weird: Pigeon

INVERTEBRATES

MOLLUSC   ECHINODERMS   COELENTERATES   ARTHROPODS

Geoduck

Top Snail

Sea Urchin

Jellyfish

ARACHNIDS   CRUSTACEANS   INSECTS   MYRIAPODS

Shrimp

VERTEBRATES

PISCES   AMPHIBIANS   REPTILES   BIRDS   MAMMALS

Yellowtail

Trout

Escolar

Pollock

Smelt

Cod

Tuna

Flying Fish

Turtle

Pigeon

Duck Balut

INDIA

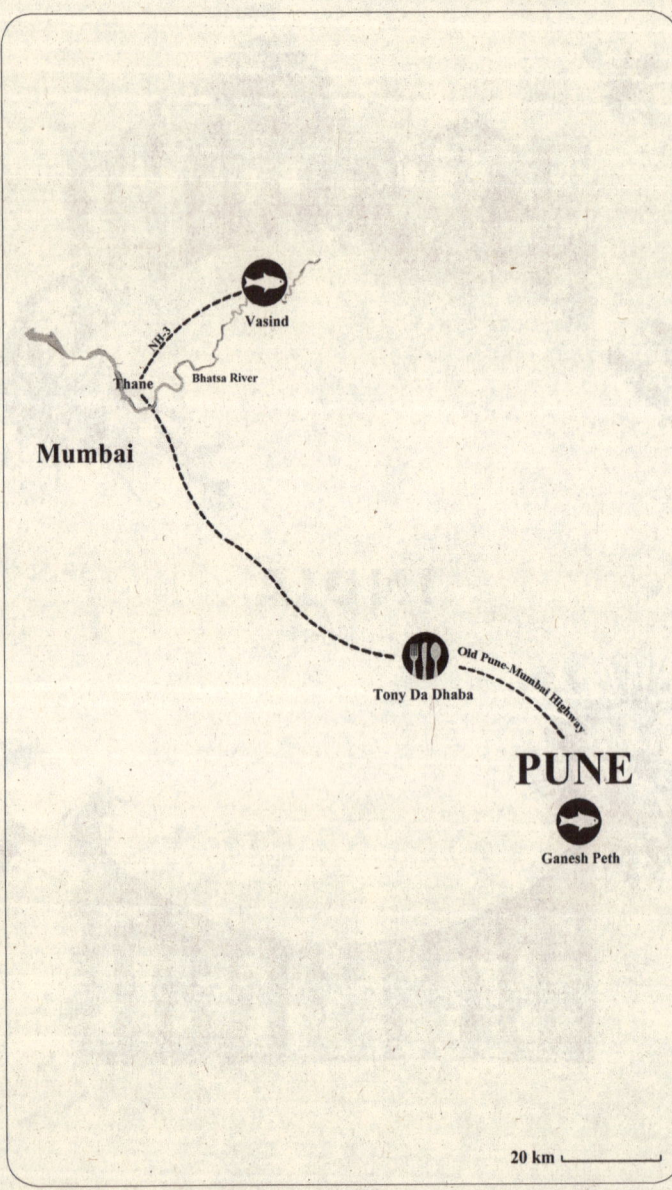

Vasind

NH-3

Thane

Bhatsa River

Mumbai

Tony Da Dhaba

Old Pune-Mumbai Highway

PUNE

Ganesh Peth

20 km

We travel around the world looking for bizarre foods to eat, but our hearts will always remain firmly back home. We each come back from our travels craving our comfort foods, mutton *rogan josh* for Vivek and thayir saadam for me. Our cross-country marriage has allowed us to experience a small portion of the culinary diversity in India, be it *elai saapadu*[*] for Vivek or *sattu*[†] for me. However, even after all this time, we've barely scratched the surface. It's impossible to compile a list of bizarre foods around the world and not include India. The diversity of soil type, climate, culture and ethnic groups across the country have resulted in diverse cuisines.

While Vivek visited me in Seattle, he was living in Pune. He was inspired by the discoveries in Seattle to find even more new species in Pune. Later, we moved to Bangalore where he continued with his explorations. Our explorations in these cities have shown us that it's very easy to find exotic varieties of food within any city in India.

---

[*] Meals served on a banana leaf
[†] A flour made by roasting grains or grams

And Then There Were None

The best way to find the freshest fish is to go where the fishmongers go. Vivek questioned many fishmongers in Pune and discovered that Ganesh Peth fish *mandi* is the best wholesale market for fish. Vivek wanted to explore it and convinced a group of friends to be a part of this expedition so that they could combine forces and buy fish in wholesale quantities.

Mithila and Piyush were the easiest to convince. They had already joined Vivek in enjoying fancy meat jerky sourced from the US, made of bison, elk, kangaroo and other exotic meats. They were excited to explore the mandi and find new seafood species in Pune. They also invited Jayant and Kaushik, two fish-loving Bengalis. The five of them decided they would have a fish barbecue. Mithila, Kaushik and Jayant were colleagues who shared Vivek's love for food—the group often talked about their food discoveries during lunch at work. Piyush is Mithila's husband and also a great chef. He played a major role in cooking many of the packaged delicacies Vivek brought back from Seattle. In true corporate style, the group assigned tasks amongst themselves. Piyush was in charge of sourcing coal for the barbecue grill that Mithila had purchased. Vivek sourced kerosene from the market through someone who had a ration card. Kaushik was in charge of driving the group to the market at 4 a.m. and Jayant said he would buy sausages as backup food in case the market expedition was unsuccessful.

On Saturday, this enthusiastic group of food adventurers drove towards Ganesh Peth market.

'Oh! There's a pet store,' said Mithila to Piyush, a few minutes into the drive. 'We should visit this later today to get a fish.'

The group was stunned.

'Mithila, there's no reason to source fish from a pet store! Even as a backup,' exclaimed Vivek in shock.

'WHAT!' exclaimed Mithila. 'I wasn't planning to eat the fish! I've been looking to buy another fish for our aquarium. Our goldfish needs a friend.'

The car ride was supposed to take forty-five minutes but took longer as there were many missed turns before they were finally able to find the market. As they got closer to Ganesh Peth, the roads became narrower. Finally, they decided that it would be better to find a parking spot and walk to the market. It was a pleasant morning and everyone enjoyed the stroll in the rising sun. They followed their noses to easily locate the market.

A lane of fish stalls marked the way to the market entrance. Ganesh Peth is a large enclosed compound that is of the size of a football field. Stalls are set up in columns within the enclosure. The stalls are much larger than regular roadside stalls. They carry bigger fish in bigger quantities than most city dwellers typically find. As Pune is a landlocked city, the fish at Ganesh Peth come in trucks early in the morning from all over the country. They saw the last few trucks enter the market and many large blue crates being unloaded. Workers were busy emptying the fish and other seafood from the crates to set up their stalls at the market.

'They had eels the size of humans or maybe even double that,' said Vivek to me later as he described their experience. 'There were at least fifty different varieties of fish and some shops also had a minimum limit on the quantity you purchased. We ensured we qualified for the minimum limit and bought as many species as we could!'

They purchased about 1–2 kilograms each of tilapia, eel, sole and prawns, then picked up a bunch of crabs that kept trying to climb out their polythene packets. Lastly, they picked up their prize of the day—a whole baby shark that weighed just over a kilogram. At stalls where the vendors demanded they buy larger quantities of fish, they pretended they were there on behalf of a larger establishment and that they were purchasing samples that would be used to determine whether they would place a larger order.

Once they were outside the market, they found some vendors to cut and chop the fish.

'It's not like cutting an onion with a kitchen knife,' Vivek has said to me many times, in an attempt to convince me that we need a butcher knife at home. However, I'm wary of experimenting with knives. I've seen half my vegetarian family and friends cut themselves while attempting to cut vegetables with their latest experiment, the ceramic knife. I definitely didn't want a weapon like the butcher knife in my kitchen. Vivek was therefore glad to discover that there were vendors outside the market who would complete this task for them. In addition to ensuring Vivek continues to have his fingers, I am helping these vendors earn their livelihood as well. To save time, the group split into two so they could get their haul cut and cleaned at two different stalls simultaneously. They were

impatient to finish with the cutting and get home to the main
task of barbecuing (and eating) all of the seafood.

~

At home, a barbecue was set up in the balcony of Vivek's
seventh-floor apartment. The balcony had a ceiling which
was two floors high and was the best surrogate to an outdoor
barbecue. Kaushik took charge of lighting the barbecue.
Piyush began marinating the fish. Vivek and Mithila were the
sous chefs, who did the cutting and chopping of the coriander,
tomatoes and onions that would go with the fish.

It took Kaushik a few attempts to manage to light and
stabilize the fire for the barbecue. He tried many different
things in his attempt—coal, pieces of fire starter, some
kerosene and old newspapers. At one point, a burning
newspaper went flying through the air and nearly set the
apartment on fire! Thankfully, they soon had a good fire
going and the first few pieces of fish and prawn were set on
the barbecue.

'It smelled amazing,' said Vivek when describing the
barbecue. 'I've always believed that what one grows or catches
oneself tastes the best. I think this is because taste is more in the
mind than on the tongue.'

I couldn't resist but cheekily point out that they hadn't
really caught the fish they barbecued.

'But the efforts in procuring that fish were no less than
catching the fish ourselves. When I tasted those first few
prawns that Piyush and Kaushik barbecued in butter, they
were better than any prawns I've ever eaten. And everyone
else agreed with me,' said Vivek.

Eel on the grill

The barbecue was done using a coal-fire, which added a smoky flavour to all the food. It brought back memories for Vivek, who has eaten food cooked directly on the fire in his village, Khudiya, near his hometown of Gorakhpur. The smokiness makes your nostrils welcome the food and dollops of nostalgia heighten the taste. The prawns were the first off the barbecue.

Next came the eels, which were the crowd pleaser of the day. They had got a medium sized eel cut into smaller cubes of around two inches in length and breadth. Eels are soft yet firm, with a slightly sweet taste. The marinade further added to the flavour.

The scariest of the seafood was the shark. The ones in the market were like the ones on TV, with fins and gills and the signature shark body. Imagine a *Jaws*-sized shark shrunk to about 1–2 feet in length. It made them feel like they were the ones who were the top predators, not the shark. The meat was dense. It tasted less like fish and more like the meat of a mammal.

As the day went by, the group continued their barbecue. One by one, eel, shark and all the other fish they sourced were consumed. The 'day' went on until midnight. Word spread and other friends joined the feast at different points during the day. But the core group of Vivek, Kaushik, Jayant, Mithila and Piyush were going strong until all the food, coal and kerosene ran out at midnight.

Ganesh Peth Market, 281–282 Ganesh Peth Road		
Item	*Barbecued Shark*	*Barbecued Eel*
Taste	★★★★★	★★★★★
Price	Rs 200/kg	Rs 200/kg
Fear Factor	4	3
New Species	Shark	Eel

Recipe: Barbecued Fish

Ingredients
Fish (of your choice), preferably sourced from a wholesale fish market
Marinade ingredients—masalas, coriander, curry leaves
Salt and pepper to taste
Butter
Cooking oil
Spades of enthusiasm for 4 a.m. drives

Method
Find the largest wholesale fish market in your city. If you don't know where this is, speak to as many retail fish vendors as you can and pick the one that's recommended the most

Find a group of like-minded friends to help you buy, cook and devour the spoils. Ensure that at least one person in this group is an excellent cook and has a secret marinade recipe.

Set up a barbecue grill.

Barbecue, eat and enjoy!

Down by the River

A few weeks after the barbecue, Vivek told me he was going on a fishing trip with his friend Saurav in Vasind, near Mumbai. While I don't like missing out on food adventures, I was thankful to skip this one. I had gone on a fishing trip with Vivek during our honeymoon in the Maldives and accidentally caught a banana fish. That poor banana fish eventually became soup and the memory continues to haunt me.

Vivek and Saurav drove to Vasind. Once they left the city, the drive took them deeper into smaller towns and villages. In Vasind, they drove until they reached the riverside. They were staying at 'Big Red Tent', a camp-stay location, where they would spend the weekend in tents by the riverside. By the time they reached it was evening, so they spent the rest of the day chatting with the host, Wayne Brown, while feasting on chai and pakodas. Wayne is a camper at heart who owns the properties on the campgrounds. He told them that he took guests on kayaking, fishing and safari trips. They were excited about going fishing and asked him about it.

'You can try, but this isn't the right season,' Wayne said. 'People have been sitting around all day without a catch. The fishing season is after the first monsoon when the river is in full flow and the fish climb up to the river banks to lay eggs in the paddy fields.'

The alternative was to go spearfishing, a night-time activity. Fishermen wade into the water with torches and spears. They shine the torch into the river, directly into the eyes of the fish. This temporarily stuns the fish and allows them to easily spear them. Neither Vivek nor Saurav had been spearfishing before, so they decided to skip fishing during the day. They spent the day kayaking instead. I didn't know it at the time, but this experience and Vivek's new-found kayaking skills would be of great use to me later. That night, they headed to the river with the villagers to try their luck at spearfishing.

They each had a spear in one hand and a torch in the other. They walked until they were chest deep in water. It was creepy. They could see only a small patch of river water with their torches. They had many false alarms where they thought they saw something, but it turned out to be a trick of the light. Despite the false alarms they began the evening with, they were able to catch a sizeable crab after which they ended the spearfishing expedition. They decided to have it for lunch the next day and asked Wayne to have it cooked for them.

The next morning, Saurav and Vivek decided that relaxing and having the crab for lunch would be a more productive use of their time during the day. They had wanted to go fishing, but there was no need to do something that had already been tested by other visitors, especially when the success rate was zero. Not ones to take no for an answer, Vivek decided to speak with the villagers they'd befriended to find alternates to angling. One of these new-found friends told him about a different method for fishing during the summer, which Vivek refers to as the 'bush and bedsheet' method.

Villagers gather bushes and roll them into a cylindrical shape, about 4–5 feet in length and 1–2 feet in width. This is set inside the water by the bank. Over the next few days, fish begin to make this bush their home. When the villagers are ready to harvest the fish, they go to the bush with a large bedsheet and toss the whole bush into it. The fish living in the bush aren't able to get out fast enough and are caught. Once the bush has been emptied off the fish, they plant it back again for the next cycle.

Bush and bedsheet: A new way to fish

This harvesting happens once a week. Vivek convinced the villagers to switch the time of their harvest and do it on the same day. They found a group of four to take them on an expedition. Two people would hold the bedsheet and the other two would pull out the bush with a quick movement and throw it into the bedsheet. Once the bedsheet is brought to the bank and the fish attempt to escape the bush, they're caught. Any smaller fish and shrimp are thrown back into the water so that they can be harvested later when they're of a size worth eating.

Snail: Caught

As this process was going on, Vivek noticed a big river snail trying to ascertain its place in the new world within the bedsheet. The locals weren't interested in a single snail and wanted to throw it away, but Vivek had been hoping to eat snails for a while. Restaurants in India don't serve snails, even if they claim to serve French cuisine where *escargot* is a delicacy. He decided this was his best shot and immediately put it into his pocket so he could take it back home and cook it. Since all slugs are not edible, he checked with some local fisherfolk if this particular variety could be eaten. They also caught some local varieties of medium-sized fish and some shrimp that were too small to be eaten. As they already had the crab from the previous night for lunch, they let the locals keep the fish they caught. After this expedition, it was time for them to head back.

~

Vivek took a lot of effort to keep the snail he'd caught alive on the drive home because he was keen to eat a fresh snail. Vasind to Pune was a four-hour car journey and he wanted to be sure that the snail wouldn't die in the heat. So, he kept the snail wet through the journey. He somehow managed to get home with a live snail. He decided to share the snail with Mithila and Piyush. The three of them had already planned to eat packaged insects that Vivek had sourced on a trip to Seattle earlier. Now, the freshly caught river snail was added to the menu. He invited them over for dinner the next day.

To ensure that the snail survived, he set up a mini ecosystem for it. He used water from a tap that provided non-chlorinated water. He ensured the snail had enough organic food to last a day. Unfortunately, the dinner was postponed for another two days. But Vivek didn't give up on his plans to harvest, cook and eat a fresh snail. Even though he had a full-time job and lived alone, he checked on the snail multiple times a day and ensured it was well fed, safe and alive.

Mithila and Piyush arrived two days later, on a Wednesday evening. They had a great evening. Many packets of salted silkworms, mealworms and scorpions were eaten. Vivek also chopped onions, tomatoes and curry leaves to fry with the snail. Even though it was just one snail, Vivek knew this would be an experience because he'd caught the snail himself.

But when the time came to fry the snail, Vivek couldn't bring himself to kill it. His desire to eat the new species was outweighed by the emotional attachment he'd developed with his newfound pet. Perhaps it was reverse Stockholm Syndrome.

'I just couldn't kill it,' he told me the next day.

'I could've told you that, but you wouldn't have believed me,' I said.

'I don't want a pet. Piyush and Mithila were looking forward to eating it, so I gifted it to them. I put it in a small box lined with wet paper and asked them to take it home and cook it.'

'Okay, so the effort wasn't totally wasted. Are you sure they have the guts to kill it?' I asked.

'Of course! They're cold-blooded enough to be able to carry out the deed. They said they'd cook it for lunch today.'

It was well past lunchtime, so I asked him if he'd spoken with them.

'Yes, I called and asked them.'

'And?'

'Apparently, it escaped.'

'WHAT!'

'Yes, it ran away into the night!'

Who Lays the Dragon Eggs?

The Department of Animal Husbandry encourages a wide variety of poultry and animal husbandry—rabbits, emu, quail, duck, guinea fowl and turkey included. Despite this, it is rare to see most of these in menus across the country. Vivek's long-time hope is to start and encourage businesses around these 'newer' species. For now, he encourages farmers by discovering and eating their wares.

As he read more about poultry and animal husbandry in India, he discovered that he lived close to Toni daa Dhaba, a large dhaba on the old Mumbai–Pune highway. We found, via multiple accounts of people, that exotic poultry including emu and turkey was available there. We decided that this establishment required our support at the earliest. I had recently moved to Bangalore and visited Pune on weekends. We decided to go to the dhaba for lunch on a Saturday while I was visiting. To ensure that we could do justice to their entire menu, Vivek invited a group of friends who also wanted to eat adventurously.

After about an hour of driving, we reached the dhaba. When we entered, I wondered if we had accidentally stumbled into a zoo instead of a restaurant. Toni daa Dhaba is situated in the middle of the owner's farm. Before we went into the restaurant, we decided to take a small stroll along the property.

The very first thing I spotted was the emu section. There was a large cage with 20–30 emus ambling about. Emus are tall birds, second in height only to their ostrich cousins. The emus at this farm were as tall as some of the tallest members of our group! Thanks to Vivek, I knew that the dhaba served emus, but I was not expecting to see them curiously staring at me while I stared back at them with equal curiosity.

Emu enclosure: Is this a zoo or a restaurant?

'How do they have emus in India? I thought I'd have to visit Australia to see one,' I said.

'You're surprised to see emus? You're from Tamil Nadu, the state where the emu Ponzi scheme in India originated,' laughed Vivek.

Obviously, I knew nothing about this Ponzi scheme and I didn't want to ask more questions about it in front of the emus lest we upset them, so I decided to walk forward. We came upon another large open-air space with fences, which housed turkeys. I wondered if all those fancy Thanksgiving menus in those fancy Koregaon Park restaurants sourced turkeys from Toni.

Suddenly, one of our friends pointed at some hen-like birds with round bodies strolling about in an adjoining enclosure.

'What are those strange looking birds?' he asked.

'Whoa! Those are guinea fowl,' said Vivek, our resident fauna expert. 'I didn't even know this place had them!'

I was glad we had seven people on this expedition. There were many species on this farm and being able to try all of them would require many people with large appetites. I hoped the others had planned ahead as Vivek had done and also skipped breakfast.

Across from where we were standing was a pond with many ducks. While the rest of the group and I looked at all the animals out of curiosity, Vivek was busy cataloguing them because he knew this was a live menu. He also told me that his online research had indicated that there was a secret item that's only available to those in the know who ask about it. He was using this walk to confirm that the species was available. It all seemed very clandestine, like those hidden speakeasy bars that require a password to enter.

'Toni daa Dhaba offers rabbits,' whispered Vivek. 'They don't list it on their menu, so you need to specifically request for it.'

'Toni daa Dhaba is like Starbucks! They never tell you they have a secret "short" size and these guys don't tell you they have a "secret" ingredient,' I retorted.

Suddenly, Vivek pointed at some cages in the distance. He suspected they were housing the elusive rabbits. The cages were of the same size and shape as those of a chicken coop, with jute sacks for roofs. Unlike chicken coops, they were covered from all sides, ostensibly to keep the contents comfortable in the shade during the blazing summer afternoon. We walked up to the cages and peered in. Almost immediately, we were able to confirm his suspicion—there were two rabbits nibbling on some greens in a corner. Vivek now knew what he would order that day and we walked to the restaurant.

Toni daa Dhaba lives up to its name with dhaba-style setting and ambience. We found a charpoy and some benches for our group and promptly settled in. The menu offered a wide range of delicacies like emu egg omelette, guinea chilli fry, emu tikka, *bater** tandoori etc. The group began discussing what they should eat. Even though it was a large group, they still didn't know how they would taste everything. The prioritization of species to eat was an exercise in optimization.

As is always the case when non-vegetarians choose their dishes, non-vegetarian food topped eggs, which topped paneer, which topped all other vegetarian food. In this case, exotic non-vegetarian meats were topping the standard options. And the secret exotic meat topped everything. So Vivek immediately asked the server if rabbit was available.

'Yes, sir,' he confirmed. 'But you will need to buy a whole rabbit. We weigh it and charge by the kilogram. Cooking is free.'

'Okay,' Vivek replied. 'How much does it cost?'

'It's Rs 2,500 per kilogram, sir,' said the server.

At that price, rabbit was the most expensive meat Vivek would ever eat, but he wasn't going to miss this opportunity.

The server also tried cross-selling an emu egg omelette to the group. We expected a large omelette given the size of the emus. However, even we were surprised by its size. The

---

* Hindi word for quail

egg was so large that it looked enough to serve everyone in the group twice over. Unlike chicken or duck eggs, it wasn't yellow or white. It had a greenish hue with a grainy texture and looked like something out of a movie.

Emu egg: Clearly birds evolved from dragons

'This is more like a dragon egg,' said Vivek, much to everyone's amusement.

However, since the adventurous eaters in the group had already decided their order, we left the emu egg omelette for another day.

The first dish was emu tikka. Emus are tough birds, with muscly legs and necks indicative of a bird that runs cross-country marathons on a regular basis. While we imagine that birds are always softer than mammals, this bird was tougher than mutton and the meat was red. It tasted heavenly. For many in the group, it was the first experience with adventurous eating so it lent a feeling of the exotic as they ate it.

The guinea fowl was next, spicy and dry. The meat was leaner and more packed with flavour as compared to chicken. As the flavour of chicken gets stronger when you go from chicken to a country chicken, guinea fowl goes beyond the country chicken in taste. It was also very well prepared.

Bater, or quail, was another surprise. Vivek had been hunting after it for a while in the farms alongside Pune, so he was glad to find and enjoy bater fry. The entire quail from neck to tail was fried in a tandoor. They looked like miniature barbecued chickens. They had lesser meat owing to their size, but the meat was tastier, making it worth the effort.

Quails (bater): So tiny, four of them are equal to one chicken

The highlight of the day, though, was the rabbit, which in addition to being the most exotic item on the menu was also the softest and tastiest of all the meats that were consumed.

The curry was well-marinated so the taste had permeated into every piece of the soft meat. The appearance of the dish could have fooled even the most hardcore non-vegetarians into thinking it was chicken. However, the group enjoyed taking out pieces and guessing which part of the rabbit's anatomy the piece had originated from. It was so tender that Vivek insists he would substitute chicken in every dish with rabbit.

Eating the rabbit further convinced Vivek that we should own a rabbit farm. Despite the Agricultural Department's encouragement, rabbits aren't seen on menus anywhere in India. He thinks it's easy to grow the business because all he needs to do is leave the rabbits to do what they do best—procreate. He can very easily ensure he has enough to feed himself rabbit curry on a regular basis, as well as set up a competing dhaba to serve other adventurous eaters.

Our dhaba will list the dish on the menu. It will be called 'The Rabbit Whole'.

Toni daa Dhaba, Mumbai–Pune Road, Kamshet, Naygaon				
Item	Emu Tikka	Rabbit Curry	Guinea Chilli Dry	Bater Tandoori
Taste	★★★	★★★★★	★★★★★	★★★
Price	Rs 520	Rs 2,200	Rs 1,150	Rs 495
Fear Factor	4	4	3	3
New Species	Emu	Rabbit	Guinea Fowl	Quail

Recipe: The Rabbit Whole
Piyush, our friend and expert home-chef, has helped us create the recipe for 'The Rabbit Whole'. If you don't want to head to Toni daa Dhaba, you can procure rabbit meat and cook it at home!

Ingredients
Rabbit (1 kg)
Onions
Tomatoes
Turmeric powder, red chilli powder, *garam masala*
2 tbsp black vinegar
Ginger–garlic paste
Spice-mix: *Laung*, black pepper, *dalchini*, *saunf*, white *til*, *rai*,
    tej patta
Yoghurt
Ghee

Method
Marinate the meat with turmeric, chilli powder and black
    vinegar. To get a smoky flavour, add burning charcoal
    with ghee to smoke the marinade vessel. Leave overnight.
Put oil on medium heat and add tej patta
Add onions and fry till light brown
Add ginger–garlic paste
Add tomato puree
Add ½ teaspoon of turmeric, 2 teaspoons of red chilli and 1
    teaspoon of garam masala
Add laung, black pepper and dalchini
Add the rabbit meat
Cook for an hour
Separately roast saunf, rai, white til and make a powder of the
    mixture. Mix it with yoghurt
Add the yoghurt mix in the curry and heat on a slow flame till
    well cooked
Add 3–4 teaspoons of ghee
Enjoy!

Food Heaven

Mosque Road is one of the busiest shopping hubs in Bangalore and becomes even busier during Ramadan. Even otherwise, Mosque Road is a foodie paradise due to the sheer number of restaurants. During Ramadan, this is coupled by the fact that every establishment has street-side carts and stalls with a range of dishes to break the fast with. This is when the road is at its festive best with street lights twinkling and carts serving up the famous *patthar ka ghosht*, non-veg samosas, *seekh* and *shami* kebabs, tikkas, prawns, *haleem*, *shahi* toast, *kheema*, *paya*,[*] korma, biryani and other mouth-watering delicacies. It was mandatory that we took time out to visit Mosque Road at *iftaar*. Vivek spent two years in Lucknow and till date his comfort food is mutton thanks to Tunday's kebabs. He was very sure that the patthar ka ghosht at Mosque Road would melt in his mouth.

So we set out to Mosque Road. It was chock-a-block with people and the stalls on both sides of the road were full. Huge crowds jostled in a haphazard manner outside every stall. I wondered how the servers managed to keep track of the orders and money collection.

---

[*] Lamb leg

We walked to the end of the road because I'd heard from friends who'd visited earlier that a stall there was serving the best patthar ka ghosht. Before we found the stall, Vivek was distracted by another one. This stall occupied the space in front of two restaurants and had displayed a wide variety of meats, samosas, paya and more on trays. The crowd in front was busy shouting out different orders. The cashiers frantically took the order, collected the money and then produced hot plates of food. We waded to the front of the crowd. Vivek was so tempted by the display that he announced he wanted to order one of every item. I pointed out that the road was chock-a-block with food. Good sense prevailed and he ordered a lamb paya, *idiyappam* and a mutton samosa. Vivek was very happy with his loot and finished it greedily.

'This paya needed just a little more chilli,' was his verdict. 'Otherwise it's cooked to perfection and tastes like a bite of heaven!'

Mosque Road, Fraser Town		
Item	*Paya*	*Mutton Samosa*
Taste	★★★	★★★★
Price	Rs 200	Rs 150
Fear Factor	2	2
New Species	None	None

~

The patthar ka ghosht was in the adjacent stall. Patthar ka ghosht is a Hyderabadi specialty, which was prepared for the royals of the Nizam court.[6] It is traditionally made by marinating lamb pieces in curd, papaya paste, elaichi, garam masala and grilled on a hot stone. This stall had set up a slab right outside the door of the restaurant where the marinated mutton was being grilled right in front of us. The slab was six inches thick, with a raging fire burning below it. The air was thick with smoke and one could smell the masalas. It was impossible to pass by and not want to buy a plate. The whole set-up looked extremely authentic and Vivek decided it was time to get in touch with his inner Nizam and try it out.

He took his first bite and closed his eyes in joy.

'This is so well cooked, it's melting in my mouth,' he said. 'This is the best dish on the entire lane! I wish I'd eaten this first, I wasted space on all that other stuff.'

I asked him if he wanted to try out the Ramadan special haleem next but he was already quite full and wanted to save space to scope out the rest of the road, lest he miss something important.

'Let's check the stalls on the other side before I order haleem,' he said. He confidently walked towards a stall at the corner, right next to the traffic light, as if he was drawn towards it. I spotted a stall selling *phirni,* a rice pudding dessert and went to buy it.

'Oh my God! Look, there's camel!' I heard Vivek call out from somewhere to my left.

I turned, expecting to see a camel all decked up to take people on camel rides. Just as I was wondering how they were offering camel rides in the middle of the road, I saw that he was standing in front of a small stall. The stall had a slab on which they were grilling some meat.

'How much for a plate of camel?' asked Vivek gleefully, as I approached holding my plate of phirni.

That was the camel—the meat grilling on the slab.

The server turned some of the meat over and plated it for Vivek. Vivek was grinning from ear to ear as he clutched his precious plate and walked away from the stall and the bustling crowds to eat it.

Grilled camel: Serendipity in Bangalore

The camel meat was tender and flavourful as it had been well-marinated and slow cooked. Like most large animals, the meat was tough, but not as tough as that of a zebra or a horse. It tasted a lot like mutton. The slow cooking on the slab ensured that it was soft. Some parts were fatty and had the slippery texture of fat. It's healthier than other meats, as it's high in protein and low in saturated fat. Vivek enjoyed this dish because he prefers well-marinated Indian spices on meat.

He finished the camel and pronounced himself full.

Even so, on the way home he said, 'The camel was so much fun, I think I want to go back for more.'

The last time I remembered someone being this enthusiastic about a camel, it was about a camel ride in the park!

Mosque Road, Fraser Town	
Item	*Camel*
Taste	★★★★★
Price	Rs 250
Fear Factor	4
New Species	Camel

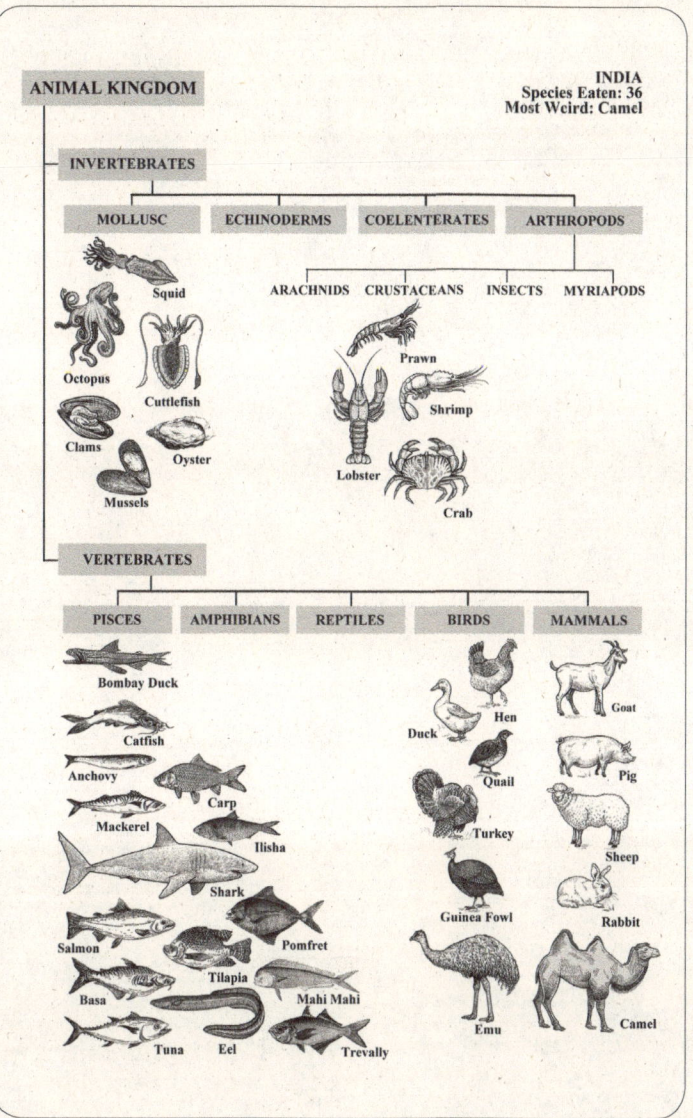

ANIMAL KINGDOM

INDIA
Species Eaten: 36
Most Weird: Camel

INVERTEBRATES

MOLLUSC   **ECHINODERMS**   **COELENTERATES**   **ARTHROPODS**

ARACHNIDS   **CRUSTACEANS**   **INSECTS**   **MYRIAPODS**

Squid

Octopus

Cuttlefish

Clams

Oyster

Mussels

Prawn

Shrimp

Lobster

Crab

VERTEBRATES

PISCES   **AMPHIBIANS**   **REPTILES**   **BIRDS**   **MAMMALS**

Bombay Duck

Catfish

Anchovy

Carp

Mackerel

Ilisha

Shark

Salmon

Pomfret

Basa

Tilapia

Mahi Mahi

Tuna   Eel   Trevally

Duck   Hen

Quail

Turkey

Guinea Fowl

Emu

Goat

Pig

Sheep

Rabbit

Camel

UNITED
KINGDOM

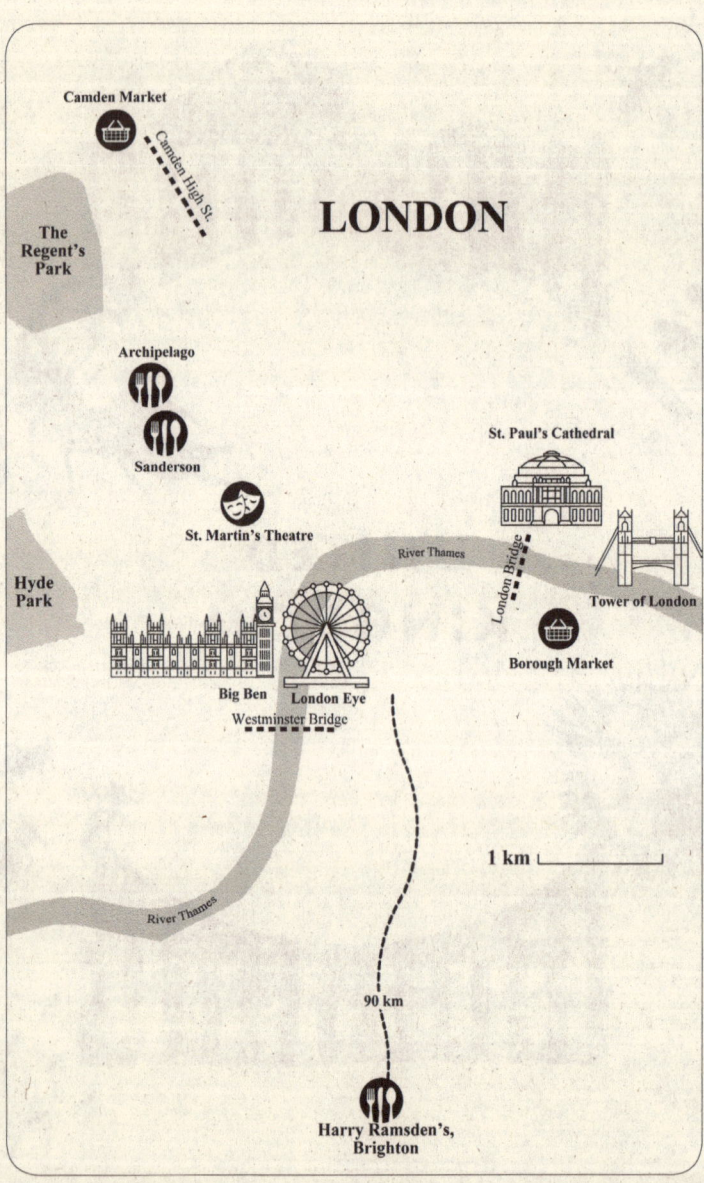

LONDON

Camden Market

Camden High St.

The Regent's Park

Archipelago

Sanderson

St. Martin's Theatre

St. Paul's Cathedral

River Thames

London Bridge

Tower of London

Hyde Park

Big Ben

London Eye

Borough Market

Westminster Bridge

River Thames

1 km

90 km

Harry Ramsden's, Brighton

The United Kingdom is packed with pulsating cities and expansive countryside locations. Each country—be it England, Wales, Scotland or Northern Ireland—is a destination in its own right and travels across the region showcase the distinctive local culture and flavours of the UK.

I needed to visit London in October 2015, for the CHI Play* design conference where I was presenting a poster. Vivek decided to accompany me, as his friends Gaurav and Richa lived in London and we could stay with them. We decided to take some time off and spend twelve days in London—one of the world's most visited cities for good reason. There's really no other city where it's possible to travel in time so seamlessly, from the Victorian era architecture of the Tower of London and Westminster Abbey to the modern architectural grandeur of the Shard Building and the Garden Bridge. It is a city of imagination with innovations in theatre, contemporary art, poetry, writing and design. What other city could claim to lend itself to bringing up a song everywhere you walk? Be it the Beatles' 'Fool on the Hill' while you walk up Primrose Hill, 'London Calling' by the Clap, Adele's 'Hometown Glory', or Elton John's 'Across the River Thames'.

London is also deeply multicultural and is one of the world's most cosmopolitan cities. The diversity infuses daily

---

* CHI (Computer Human Interface) Play conference is an international interdisciplinary conference for areas of play, games and human-computer interaction.

life, fashion, music and food. Whether it's the museums like the British Museum and Victoria and Albert Museum with their diverse collections or the flavours at the Borough Market that are from all over the world, London is a melting pot of influences.

English cuisine incorporates ingredients and ideas from Africa, India and China, from the colonial era as a result of post-war immigration. London showcases almost every cuisine. The traditional English meals include bread and cheese, roasted meats, savoury meats and game pies, broths, and freshwater and saltwater fish. I was excited to try out scones, clotted cream, anchovies, cucumber sandwiches and all the other local delicacies that had piqued my interest as a child devouring Enid Blyton's books. Vivek, on the other hand, was excited about heading out to the quintessential London markets that offer a mind-blowing variety of dishes. During our trip, we had enough time to see the sights and eat many local and international dishes.

A Pound of Flesh and More

Borough Market is London's largest and oldest food market, dating back to the twelfth century.[7] Set right next to the financial district, it has food stalls with vendors from around the world displaying their wares, making it a great place to find specialty food.

Our first trip to the market was on our first day; we headed there for a late lunch. Borough Market has over a hundred shops selling gourmet foods ranging from cheese and chocolate to baked goods and exotic meats. The quaint buildings in and around the market add to its charm. The closed enclosure has arched awnings and is filled with shops along the aisles, that have displays advertising their products. In the centre of the enclosure are the multiple tables selling foodstuff.

The food there was also displayed in the most enticing manner, making you want to buy things you don't even think you'd like. I spotted a cheese exhibit from Norway with wedges of cheese arranged in a pyramid-like fashion that I immediately purchased. We soon realized that coming to the market late in the afternoon was a bad idea because it shuts at 5 p.m. on Saturdays and opens early, around 8 a.m. It was an hour away from closing time and most vendors had run out of stock. Some had already shut their stalls.

Vivek isn't one to be daunted by mundane things such as time, so we walked through the market to get a sense of what was on offer. There are many alleys and we explored each one to find the best of Borough. We'd taken about three circuits of the market and had almost given up on finding anything, because there was barely anything left to find, when we stumbled upon an alley we missed earlier. It was tucked away behind a corner that looked like a dead-end. We only had about ten minutes left before the market shut but we still headed there.

'Even if the stalls are shut, maybe I can chat with the owners,' Vivek said.

We went into the alley and discovered a shop with a large handwritten sign advertising their special, 'KANGAROO SKEWERS'. Vivek jumped up and down like he was a kangaroo himself and ran towards it. He quickly struck up a conversation with the owner and discovered that she also sold crocodile, zebra and other game meats from South Africa. Everything was sold out for the day, except the kangaroo skewers, which she was barbecuing to serve.

'If you eat kangaroo skewers here, what will you eat when we visit Australia?' I asked him.

'A kangaroo in hand is worth two in the bush,' he quipped. 'I will find some other species there. I'm sure they have more than enough.'

There were three kangaroo meatballs on a bamboo skewer. The kangaroo meat tasted like lamb but was much deeper in flavour. It was leaner and low in fat. It was juicy and well cooked. While the animal is so cute that you may want to skip eating it, it's tasty enough to deserve a try! Vivek decided to come back to locate more such treasures.

Borough Market, 8 Southwark Street	
Item	*Kangaroo Skewers*
Taste	★★★
Price	£5
Fear Factor	4
New Species	Kangaroo

~

Before our next visit to Borough Market, we visited Camden Market. Camden is a large retail market that sells crafts, clothing, bric-a-brac and food. At the entrance arcade of Camden, we spotted Shaka Zulu, a restaurant that served many varieties of game meat. We skipped it because it was pricey and Vivek was convinced that another round of searching through Borough Market would yield similar results at a better price. Instead, we tried the falafels from the food area. These falafels were as good as the ones in the Middle East, the benchmark with which I evaluate all falafels.

As we wandered through the market we stumbled upon Chin Chin Labs, an ice cream shop that specializes in nitrogen ice cream, in an alley off the main arcade. The process of making nitrogen ice cream is so intriguing that many ice cream makers who use this technique are like performance artists. The resultant ice cream is creamier than regular ice cream. Chin Chin Labs also has a range of madcap flavours ranging from Bee Pollen Honeycomb to Lychee Rose Coconut to Burnt Butter Caramel.

I chose the Valrhona Dark Chocolate, a classic flavour instead of the experimental ones. The flavour was spot-on—the bitter dark chocolate was not overpowered by sweetness.

Any trip to Camden Market cannot be complete without a stop at Chin Chin Labs.

~

While in London, I also wanted to have British high tea, a decadent afternoon meal laden with savouries, sweets and tea, mostly because years of reading Enid Blyton had made me curious about scones, clotted cream and pies. I combined this with my love for *Alice in Wonderland* and we landed up at the Sanderson Hotel for the Mad Hatters' Afternoon Tea, a traditional British high tea that's set up with an *Alice in Wonderland* theme.

It was an elaborate spread. The table décor was themed *Alice in Wonderland*, with the various teas labelled 'Drink Me'. The cake and pastry stand was, of course, labelled 'Eat Me'. The entire set up had the effect of making us feel like we had really tumbled down the rabbit hole and landed at the Mad Hatter's table. The savouries included smoked salmon, quail eggs with caviar, ham and parmesan sandwiches, cucumber sandwiches and a Cornish crab roll. The pastries included scones and clotted cream, macarons, meringues and other goodies. My favourites were the cucumber sandwiches, which tasted every bit as good as I'd imagined, and the meringues. The tea selection was also really good and I enjoyed the citrusy orange white tea that I tried.

~

Over the weekend, Vivek's friend Gaurav suggested we visit Brighton, a small beach town near London. Brighton is a fashionable seaside resort with many Victorian-era architectural buildings including the Grand Hotel, the West Pier and the Brighton Place pier. It's also famous for graffiti, including Banksy's 'Kissing Coppers' located on the side of the Prince Albert Pub.

We took the train to Brighton, an hour-long journey from King's Cross Station in London. Once we got there, we walked from the station to the beach to soak in the town. It was a beautiful walk with many pubs and restaurants on the way. We got to the beach and decided to find a pub by the water so we could enjoy the view. We sat there for a while chatting and eating finger food while watching the sunset. We had barely decided we should head out for dinner when Vivek came up with a recommendation.

'Let's go to Harry Ramsden's,' he said. 'It's a ninety-year-old restaurant and recommended quite highly.'

I knew there was more to this restaurant than just being an old establishment with good reviews, but we had to eat so I didn't question Vivek's ulterior motives behind wanting to go. It was close to the station so we could dine and dash (after paying!) if we needed to. Once we got there, Vivek didn't even need the menu because he had already looked it up online. He asked if Swordfish Steak was available. He was in luck that day!

The Swordfish Steak was huge and grilled well. It was an English fish and chips dish, with fried swordfish and thick potato wedges. Vivek looked at the giant portion and immediately decided he would prioritize the steak. I was able to claim all the chips. The steak was tough, possibly the toughest fish he's eaten. It was also dense and left him fuller than what he expected. He loved it and made sure to leave nothing on his plate but the bones. Vivek credited the seaside air for his ability to work up the appetite for this giant fish.

The mighty swordfish

We finished dinner with about fifteen minutes left for the last train to London. We rushed out to take a tram and then ran all the way to the platform. Vivek had his excitement for the day in the form of the swordfish and the rest of us got ours in that sprint where we were wondering if we would make it.

Harry Ramsden's, 1–4 Marine Parade	
Item	*Swordfish Steak*
Taste	★★★
Price	£10.95
Fear Factor	3
New Species	Swordfish

~

The next day, we were back at Borough Market with plenty of time to spare. Early on, I stocked up pastries from the bakeries that are located in the central space of the market. I was busy munching on this stash while Vivek poked about in all the corners and alleyways of the market. If there's one thing I've learnt while travelling with him, it's to bring along enough snacks of my choice for the walks!

Borough Market bakery

We went ahead and found our kangaroo seller friend from our previous trip. This time, she had an extensive display of game meats available, most of which were ready for purchase and cooking at home. Some meats were available as skewers, already cooked. Vivek got two skewers—one with zebra meat and the other a mix of zebra, ostrich and kangaroo.

The zebra meat was very fibrous in texture, which Vivek says is a common characteristic of meat from larger animals. It was also light and low in fat. He liked the kangaroo best. He expected ostrich to taste more like a regular bird and have softer meat, but it was coarser in texture and closer to other mammals, reminding him of its cousin, the emu.

The Bigger Mac: Kangaroo, zebra, buffalo, ostrich and
crocodile patties

Mammal, bird, marsupial

Later, I discovered that London is the best place in the world to try African game meat since it was banned for consumption in Africa in early 2000.[8] South Africa exports the meat from animals that aren't endangered and the UK is one of its primary markets. For anyone interested in African game meat, Borough Market is the best destination.

As he devoured the skewers, he launched into an extensive conversation with the storeowner to find out what else was available.

'I have raw horsemeat,' she said, pointing at the large fridge behind her.

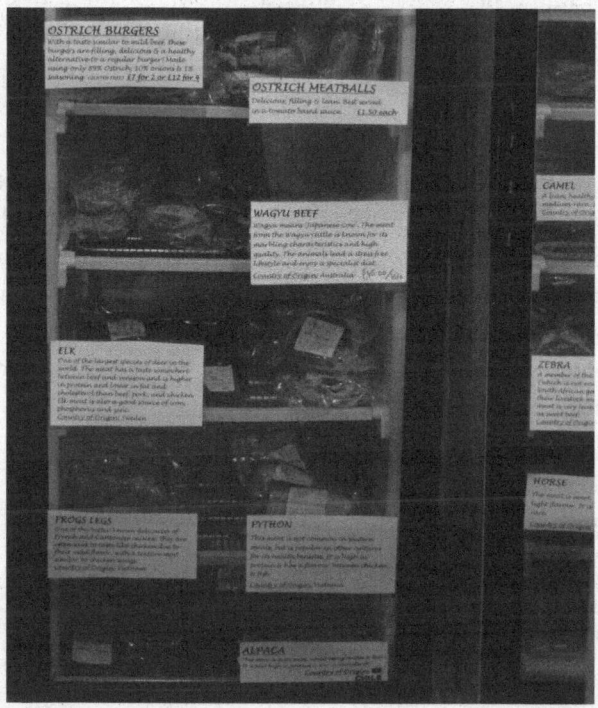

Frog, elk, python, alpaca, horse and camel in the fridge

Vivek peered into her fridge and was thrilled to see it was stocked with much more than horsemeat. She also had elk, crocodile, frog, python, alpaca, camel and a variety of other meats sourced from all over the planet. These were in varying forms ranging from steaks to burger patties. His prayers were answered.

'That's perfect,' he said. 'I need to get the horsemeat right away. We have access to a kitchen!'

I reminded him that the kitchen he was referring to belonged to Gaurav and Richa, our friends. While I'm largely forgiving about what happens at my vegetarian kitchen, I didn't think they would be quite as accommodating. In order to ensure we didn't jeopardize our friendship, he walked away from the horse and the rest of the animal kingdom in that fridge. However, they all went onto his list of species to eat.

He also gave up on a goose egg that he found in a supermarket. While it seemed that boiling an egg would be an easier thing to talk our friends into, this egg was three times the size of a regular egg and would have raised too many questions. Besides, after the balut incident, I'm suspicious of eggs that originate from birds other than hens.

'I guess I can't harvest all the eggs from the golden goose at once,' he said, as we walked away.

The Exotic Meat Company, Borough Market, 8 Southwark Street		
Item	*Zebra Skewers*	*Kangaroo, Ostrich and Zebra Skewers*
Taste	★★★	★★★
Price	£5	£10
Fear Factor	4	4
New Species	Zebra	Ostrich

The Python Programme

One of London's top sights isn't really a sight but a performance. Agatha Christie's *Mousetrap* has been running at St Martin's theatre for over sixty years.[9] Despite being a huge fan, I never read the Internet spoilers. I'd long hoped that I'd visit London and have the complete experience—watch the play, find out whodunit and receive that special warning not to share the mystery. I booked tickets for one of the front rows and was behaving in a true fan-girl manner by talking about it every five minutes through the trip.

To get to St Martin's Theatre, we caught the subway to Leicester Square station, a short walk away from the theatre. As we walked, Vivek said he wanted to stop at a restaurant nearby since we had a fair bit of time before the play began. We walked through multiple by-lanes in and around Leicester Square and Piccadilly Circus. After searching for about twenty minutes, we finally found the restaurant. The restaurant, Archipelago, looked unassuming from the outside. We stepped in and were instantly entranced. It was like entering a Zen forest, with multiple plants and Buddha statues all around. The ambience convinced me that this was a vegan restaurant. Finally, we were at a restaurant where the food was right up my alley. After multiple visits to Borough Market, it was time

I got to eat some good food! I was thankful that Vivek had thought of such a good dinner date location.

The restaurant was fairly empty and the owner came over with the menus. He asked if we knew about the specialties and Vivek nodded. I was too busy looking at the menu to respond. As I scanned it, I realized a few things. One, this was not a vegan restaurant. Two, this would barely qualify as a vegetarian restaurant. In fact, even non-vegetarians would've been wary of this place. Archipelago was essentially a haven for connoisseurs of exotic meats. They were serving python, crocodile, alpaca and other mind-boggling meats. And for those who lasted until dessert, they also served chocolate covered locusts. I'm a big fan of chocolate, but I didn't plan to have it coated on locusts!

Here I was, thinking I was being treated to an amazing vegan meal and instead I was at London's top restaurant for the adventurous eater. Vivek saw the look on my face and hastened to assure me that he was taking me to another restaurant after he tasted two items on their menu—the python carpaccio and crocodile wrapped in vine leaves. I let him order these dishes and ordered a glass of juice for myself. The food arrived and both dishes looked like works of art.

The python meat was cut out like round strips of chicken salami, but had an uneven texture. The crackers looked like cutlets. The meal also included a side salad. Unlike the fibrous texture that's typical of chicken, python meat has a perfectly soft, smooth, rubber-like texture. Eating the python marked the beginning of a new branch in Vivek's food tree, the reptiles. I was certain it would soon get filled up.

The crocodile was another work of art. The meat was laid out on the vine leaves, with samphire leaves on the side. The honey poached plums added a dash of colour to the plate. The crocodile tasted like chicken *keema* spiced with something that tasted like chaat masala. It appealed to Vivek's Indian taste buds, reminding him of various Lucknowi keema dishes.

Crocodile in vine leaves

We left with enough time to spare so I could grab a bite at one of the restaurants along the way.

I was right, though. The highlight of the trip to London (for me) was watching *The Mousetrap*. While Vivek didn't eat a horse, he ate a zebra, the wilder cousin, so it was a good start.

Archipelago, 53 Cleveland Street, Fitzrovia		
Item	*Cayman Islands (Crocodile wrapped in vine leaves, honey poached plums and pickled samphire)*	*Burmese Embrace (smoked python carpaccio, green tea and wasabi crackers and puree)*
Taste	★★★★	★★★★
Price	£12	£12.50
Fear Factor	5	5
New Species	Crocodile	Python

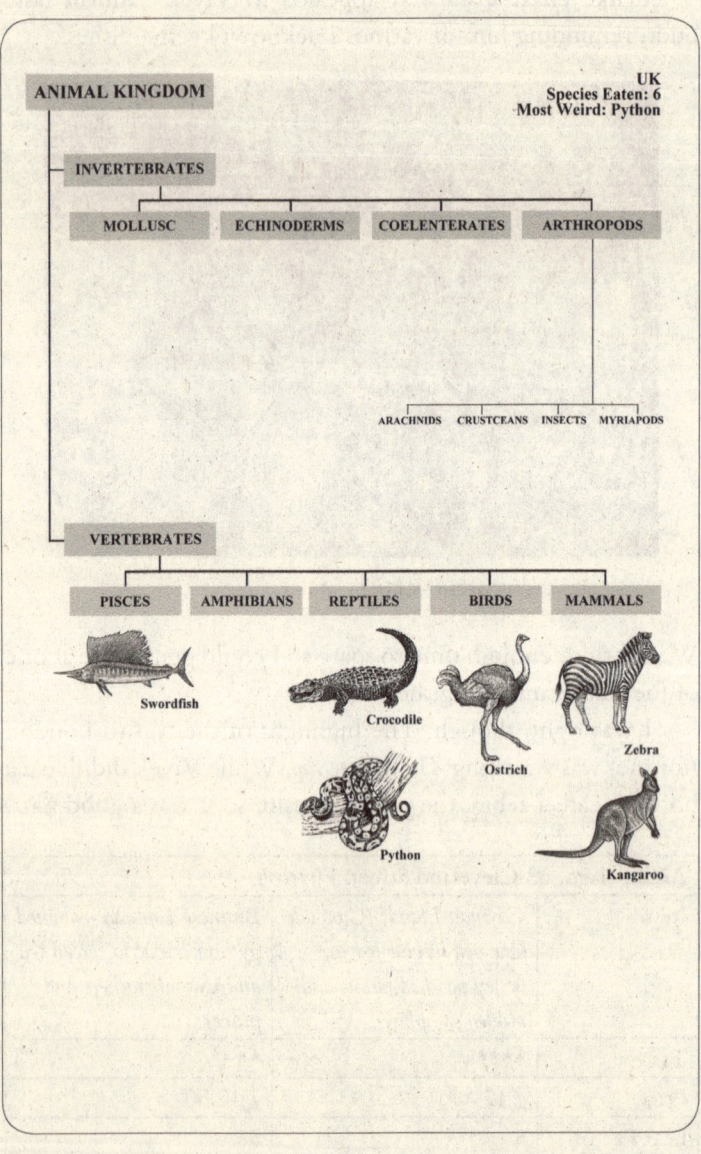

LUXEMBOURG

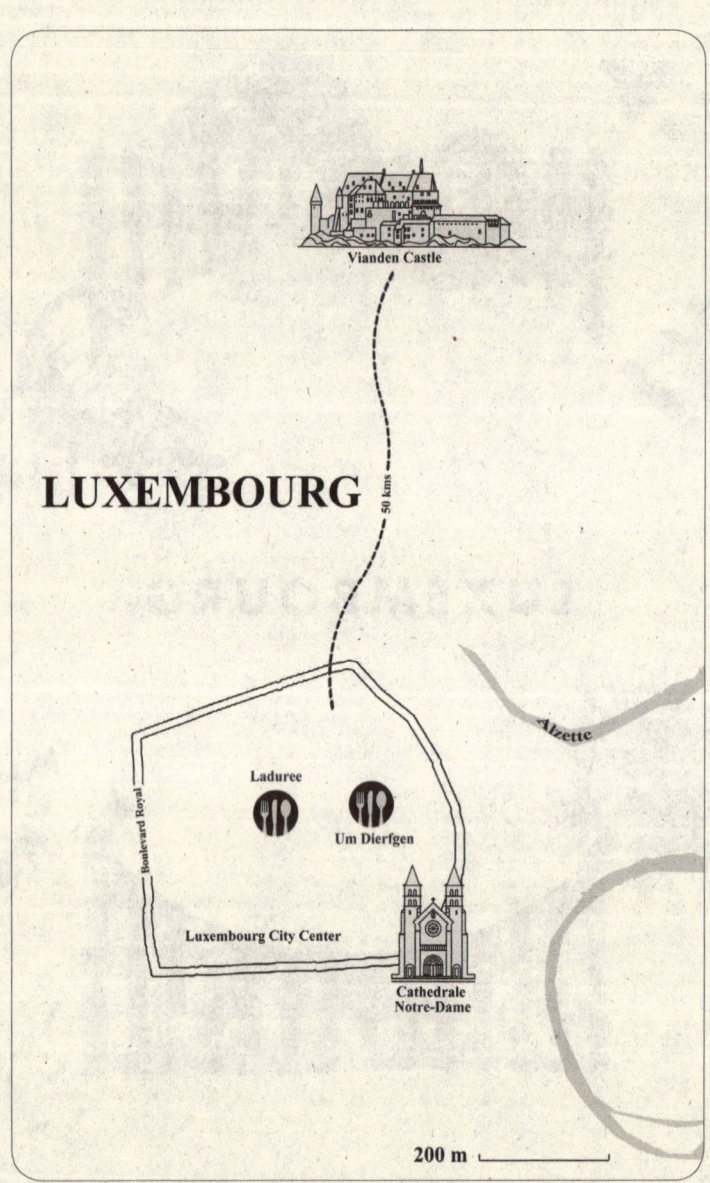

Vianden Castle

LUXEMBOURG

50 kms

Alzette

Laduree

Um Dierfgen

Boulevard Royal

Luxembourg City Center

Cathedrale
Notre-Dame

200 m

Tucked away between Belgium, France and Germany is a tiny country with a capital city straight out of a fairy tale. Luxembourg is a country full of surprises, from the vineyards of Moselle to the rock formations of the Mullerthal region, to the green valleys of Ardennes. Luxembourg City, the capital, is a UNESCO heritage site perched on a dramatic cliff top. It has an interesting dichotomy of a modern central business district that's alongside the old town with historical architecture.

Many years of foreign influences have resulted in a fairly international influence on the cuisine of the region. The local cuisine in Luxembourg is typical of the farming community lifestyle that was part of the Grand Duchy's history. Traditional dishes are *Judd mat Gardebouden* (the neck of pork cooked with broad beans), *traipen* (fried blood sausage) with applesauce and crayfish.

We visited Luxembourg in the summer of 2016 when Vivek decided to accompany me on a work trip. We spent the weekend going around the old city and visiting Vianden Castle. Vivek was able to explore more of Luxembourg during the week while I was at work. He, obviously, tried some of the local cuisine during this time.

So Hungry, I Ate a Horse

Luxembourg is a tiny country with a population of half a million people.

'I'm sure there are as many people in all of Luxembourg as there are boarding a Mumbai local on a single morning,' said Vivek while we walked around the city centre.

The city centre has a beautiful marketspace set on stone-paved streets that cross over each other. The central square is enclosed by restaurants. There are live music performances on the streets in the evenings, making this a great place for a relaxed meal. I was thrilled to discover that Laduree, the famous Parisian patisserie credited with the invention of the macaron, had an outlet here. Unlike its Parisian counterpart, the one in Luxembourg didn't have long lines inching their way into the store. I took advantage of this and bought multiple flavours of macarons like salted caramel, chocolate, orange blossom and strawberry mint. Each one was airy, light and deeply flavourful—a perfect advertisement for why Laduree is famous. I made sure to go back and buy more, including some to take home.

My other discovery was Gelateria Artiginale, one of the best gelateries I've ever visited. They had really good lemon-flavoured gelato with the perfect blend of sweet and tangy. I kept going back for it since it's very hard to find a good lemon gelato—they're almost always overly sweet and don't allow for the tang to shine through. The town square in Luxembourg was aptly placed to cater to my sweet tooth while Vivek went around experimenting with new food.

Since it was mid-August, the days were still long and it was sunny even at 7 p.m. During the week, I got back to the hotel around that time and we would take a bus to the market for dinner. At lunchtime, Vivek had to fend for himself. He knew that horsemeat was eaten in some parts of Europe and hoped to find it in Luxembourg. On the first two days, he was unsuccessful in his quest. He spent the day walking around the city centre asking the locals if they could recommend a restaurant that served horse. However, any leads he received invariably resulted in dead ends because it was one of those local dishes that wasn't on the restaurant menus catering to travellers. His quest took him towards the old quarter of Luxembourg, an area that's not frequented by tourists.

To get to the old quarter, one needs to cross a bridge over the confluence of the Alzette and Petrusse rivers that run through the city. This is a scenic walk, where you get a view of the valley below as you stroll through old-European style buildings that are all around the old quarter. As he walked through the area, he sent me pictures of the fortress, the public buildings and the churches.

One afternoon, he sent me a photo of a plate with some meat in sauce and salad on the side.

I realized that he had finally found the right restaurant, Café Um Diefergan, and this was a horse steak. Through his trips, he'd discovered that it's called '*cheval*' and this led to the discovery of the dish. It was a large piece of lean meat.

It was so muscular that he wondered if he would even be able to cut it or if he would embarrass himself. He was able to cut it and enjoyed the steak. The meat was tough and way more fibrous than anything else he'd tried till then. He remembered that there had been a major hue and cry in the UK over the fact that horsemeat was substituted for beef, indicating that its closest comparison would be beef. [10] Every bite of the horse steak was so chewy that it felt like he was fighting a real horse in his mouth.

'That must've been hard,' I said.

'Actually, it was easy,' he said. 'You see, I was so hungry, I ate a horse!'

Café Um Diefergan, 6 Cote D'Eich	
Item	*Steak de Cheval Sauce Piquante*
Taste	★★★★
Price	€25.50
Fear Factor	5
New Species	Horse

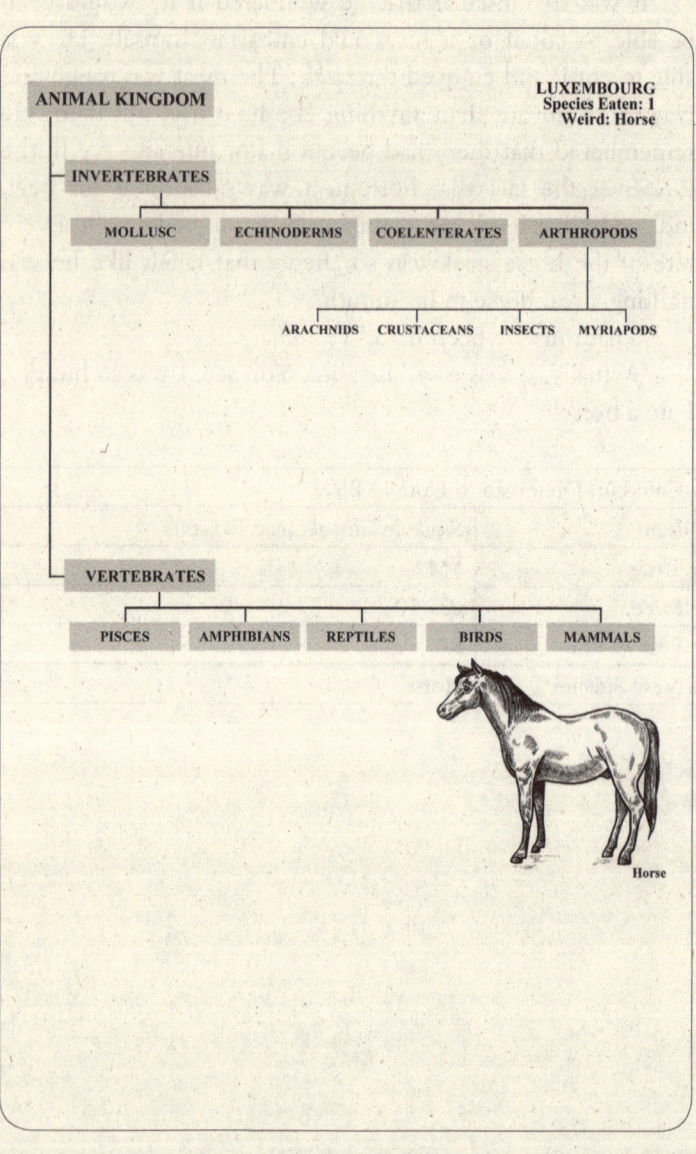

ANIMAL KINGDOM

LUXEMBOURG
Species Eaten: 1
Weird: Horse

INVERTEBRATES

MOLLUSC · ECHINODERMS · COELENTERATES · ARTHROPODS

ARACHNIDS · CRUSTACEANS · INSECTS · MYRIAPODS

VERTEBRATES

PISCES · AMPHIBIANS · REPTILES · BIRDS · MAMMALS

Horse

THAILAND

BANGKOK

Chao Phraya River

Taling Chan
Floating Market

Khao San Road

The Grand Palace

Chatuchak
Market

Chatuchak
Park

Wat Arun

Wat Pho

Phra Pokklao Bridge

Bangkok MRT

Khlong Toei
Station

Khlong Toei
Market

Chao Phraya River

2 km

Whether you're a beach person or a mountain person, a foodie or a non-foodie, whether you like adventure or lazing around, Thailand will have something for you. The popular attractions range from the beautiful beaches of Phuket, Krabi and Koh Samui to the iconic temples in Bangkok and Chiang Mai, to historical cities like Ayutthaya. Thailand is also not an expensive country to get around in, making it one of the top destinations for a quick getaway.

For us, the biggest draw to Thailand was the food. Thai cuisine is varied and flavourful. And for the adventurous foodie, it offers a variety of unusual foods ranging from insects to frogs, to snakes and more.

Thailand offers four different types of cuisine. Northern Thai cuisine showcases the influence of Laos and Myanmar, as well as from China. The food here is less salty because the salt in Thai food comes from fish sauce and seafood isn't as common in the North. It is renowned for its chilli dips. The primary tastes in the food are bitter and sour.

North-eastern Thailand is home to Isaan cuisine. The Isaan region is one of the least visited in the country because most of the region is remote. The food here is grilled, as is the case in other parts of Thailand. People in Isaan eat things that are readily available and easy to catch and hence frogs and insects are staples. The food is also less salty and spicy when compared to other parts of Thailand. While it is nearly impossible to find Isaan food outside of Thailand, it is still possible to find dishes from this region in metropolitan areas within the country, like Bangkok. The most popular dish in this region is *nam phrik bla*, a spicy fermented fish and chilli dipping sauce.

Central Thai cuisine is a blend of both the Northern and Southern styles and is milder in flavour. It is also the cuisine that's most popular outside of Thailand and includes popular dishes like pad thai and curry pastes with kaffir lime and shrimp.

Southern Thailand is where you find spicy Thai food. The flavour is most intense in this region. Fish sauce is used in most of the dishes here owing to the abundance of seafood. Curries in the South are thicker and more flavourful. They use coconut milk for the thickness, whereas the curries in the North use broth or stock. The food here also uses flavours from the neighbouring Indonesia and Malaysia.

When we first considered visiting Thailand in 2016, we wanted to head to the North and North-eastern regions, especially Isaan, for the frogs and insects. However, we only had four days and so we decided to head to Bangkok instead. We booked ourselves into an Airbnb that was close to a metro line to allow for easy accessibility to all the markets. The markets in Bangkok have vendors from all parts of Thailand, making it easy to find a sampling of all kinds of Thai food made authentically. Our trip was dedicated to eating as many new types of Thai food that we possibly could and we were delighted to try at least one dish from every region.

A Bug's Life

One of the best places to find varied styles of food in Bangkok is the night market at Khao San Road. Khao San Road is the backpacking area filled with cafes, bars and hostels. Every evening, the road transforms into a riot of colour and light as numerous street vendors set up stalls and pushcarts to sell all kinds of snacks, desserts and souvenirs. At Khao San Road, people party into the wee hours of the morning and the street vendors have a steady stream of food for the partygoers to soak up the alcohol through the night. As foodies on a mission, Khao San Road was our first destination in Bangkok. We went there late in the afternoon so we could pace ourselves and try different dishes through the evening and night.

We began by walking through Soi Rambuttri, a little alleyway parallel to Khao San Road. While Khao San Road is more famous, Soi Rambuttri gives you a glimpse of Bangkok before it became a big city with a row of restaurants and cafes on a road lined with leafy banyan trees on either side. It's quaint and feels like it is part of a city that's from another era altogether.

We spent some time walking down the road and soaking in the laidback vibe. The walk gave us a chance to build up our appetites and check out the various eating options on the road. The entrance to Soi Rambuttri on Thanon

Chakrabongse, which is closer to Khao San Road, is like a mini Khao San Road. During the day, it has colourful cafes where tourists grab drinks and wait for the sun to go down. The cafes transform into the popular party areas later in the evening with live music performances.

On the other end of Soi Rambuttri is a row of street food stalls frequented by locals. Once we saw the variety of food available there we decided to start our eating expedition from this part of town. Every street cart had large trays upfront that displayed different kinds of noodles and rice along with curries and sauces, as well as vegetables, meats and other add-ons for the soup dishes. The cooking happens on a stove set up right behind this display. While the vendors don't speak much English, this display makes it easy to assess what looks interesting and you can simply point at what you'd like to try. There are also stalls selling fresh fruit juice to go with the food.

We walked down the road, away from the Khao San entrance, until the opposite junction where we found a stall that seemed to have every possible curry-rice-noodle combination that we could have thought of and more! The stall was on the footpath and there were tables placed next to it. The tables were already filling up with locals and tourists alike, with more queuing up to take their place. We took this as a sign and decided to pick a few things.

There's a saying that when in Thailand, you have to pick which road to take—rice or noodles. It was too early in our trip to make such a big decision, so we picked both. We started with pad thai and followed it up with two types of Thai curry with jasmine rice. One was a *massaman* chicken curry and the other was a vegetable green curry. All three dishes were perfectly cooked and we savoured every bite. The pad thai was especially well flavoured with a peanut sauce that had just the right amount of sweetness in it. The vendor was generous with the chopped peanuts, which added the right amount of crunch to the dish. Of the two curries, the massaman curry was the clear winner—it was spicier and the spices were well-balanced by the coconut milk. The green curry was also very good but was overshadowed by the other two dishes.

Soi Rambuttri food carts: Making you an offer you can't refuse

Street Cart, Street Buffet area on Soi Rambuttri (Central and Southern Thai Specialty)			
Item	*Pad Thai*	*Massaman Curry*	*Thai Green Curry*
Taste	★★★★★	★★★★★	★★★★★
Price	฿30–40	฿30–40	฿30–40
Fear Factor	1	1	1
New Species	None	None	None

~

We continued our explorations in Soi Rambuttri. The other end of the road was filled with boutique cafes and pubs. Unlike the street stalls where people were eating and leaving immediately after, the patrons here were more relaxed. Many of them looked like they'd been sitting there a while and weren't likely to leave any time soon. We were looking through the menus displayed outside the restaurants to see if any of them served unusual dishes when a street vendor appeared seemingly out of nowhere. He began waving a scorpion on a stick under Vivek's nose. I instantly expected Vivek to react exactly like a child in a candy shop because one of his primary objectives was to eat insects. Contrary to my expectations, he didn't buy any. I must've looked as surprised as I felt because he explained that the vendor was fleecing him, by asking for ฿250. I was quite amused that I married the rare man who knew the right price for a scorpion on a stick! He said he would wait until after dark because Khao San Road would have many insect carts and he'd be able to find more insects and get a better deal since he would be 'buying in bulk'.

So, we left Soi Rambuttri and wandered onto Khao San Road, where we stopped at the 9 Bar while we waited for the carts to appear after sunset. We sat there for about an hour and left as soon as dusk began to fall. As luck would have it, we stumbled upon a cart almost immediately. The cart was like a pushcart you'd see with a roadside vendor in India, except that in the place of peanuts or *bhutta* or *chana choor*, there was every manner of creepy-crawly displayed in all their glory. The vendor had decided to park herself right at the beginning of Khao San Road to show off her wares. There were various insects displayed on tin trays and organized by size. The insects were segregated into various groups. The first group was insects sold by weight, like silkworms, bamboo worms, grasshoppers, beetles and the likes. You could buy a specific insect or a mixed bag. Vivek was annoyed to discover that the mixed bag included tiny frogs because he didn't appreciate the misclassification of an amphibian in a bag of insects.

The next section showcased bigger and creepier insects like centipedes, spiders and scorpions. These were more expensive and sold by the number, typically one or two, as no one seemed to want a larger quantity. Finally, we spotted something we didn't know we'd find—water snakes! It was the most expensive item at the cart and clearly meant for the discerning customer.

The cart looked so interesting that many tourists stopped by to examine it. The unusual nature of the wares also made people pull out their phones to snap a picture. But they were immediately stopped by the vendor who kept pointing at a big sign displayed right in front of the cart that said, 'PHOTO ฿10.' She continued to repeat this out loud for anyone who ignored her to make sure she wasn't cheated out of her photo income. Judging by the reactions, I'd guess there are days when she makes more money from the photos than from insect connoisseurs.

But Vivek was a serious customer. Insects have been on his radar ever since he first read about how they are the solution to the global food crisis. They are highly nutritious, often containing twice as much protein per 100g as fish and meat. Rearing insects is also more energy efficient, making them the perfect superfood.[11] Interestingly, almost one-third of the world's cultures eat insects. In addition to understanding more about eating insects, trying out many of them in one meal also gave Vivek the opportunity to add multiple species to his chart in a single outing.

He began chatting with the vendor about all the insects available. As she saw him struggle to make a choice, she immediately recommended the mixed box, priced at ฿300. The mixed box contained grasshoppers, silkworms, bamboo worms, crickets, beetles, water bugs and frogs. After a few minutes of haggling, they settled at ฿200.

He then moved on to the next section where he picked a centipede for ฿100 and a spider for ฿200. The centipede was nearly as big as his hand, with its hundred legs projecting outward and looked quite scary. I thought he'd stop, but he started looking at the snakes laid out on one of the trays.

The snake was small—it would probably be about one foot if it were straightened. It was coiled, with a skewer running through the centre in a kebab-like fashion. We couldn't understand what type of snake it was since the vendor couldn't speak much English.

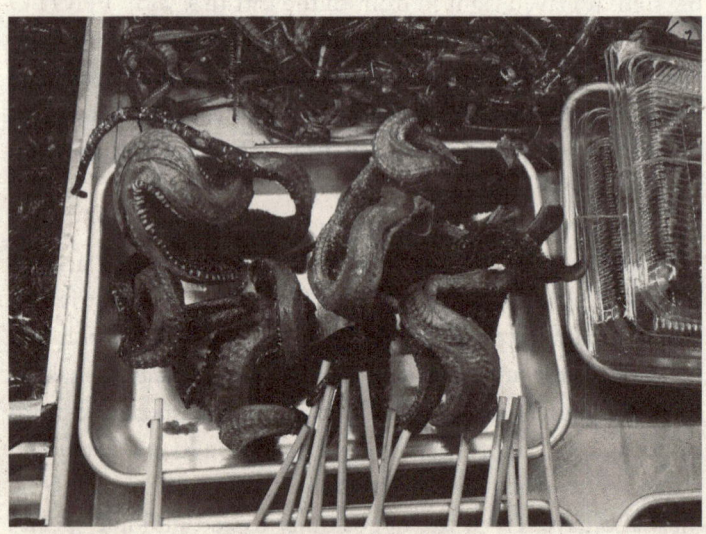

Snakes on your plate

Vivek later spent many hours matching the patterns and colours from a photo of the snake to online search image results and determined that this was a water snake. He hesitated when he heard that it cost ฿500. However, the opportunity to try a new species was too good to resist. He rationalized his spending by the discounts the vendor offered him as a premium customer. Finally, at the last stage of negotiations, we asked her if as buyers we could take photos for free and she said we could. Our deal was sealed.

Vivek started looking at each insect in his box carefully. All of these insects were eaten whole—wings, legs, eyes, antennae et al.!

The silkworms were from the pupae stage, where the silkworm forms a cocoon around itself. The exterior is crunchy but the insides were wet and squishy. Bamboo worms are larvae from the moths which live in bamboo groves. Crickets are the most commonly eaten insects. They tasted like thin potato wafers. Grasshoppers are the premier version of crickets. They're not as easily available, but they're larger, more beautiful and more nutritious than crickets. Crickets are the *bhujia* of insects and grasshoppers are the *kurkure*.

The beetles looked like works of art with beautiful, shiny bodies. Water bugs were the largest and the scariest looking of all the insects. They tasted like the monsoon bugs that accidentally land up in your mouth during a high-speed bike ride. The centipede had the most meat but was also overcooked to the point of being burnt. Vivek was very disappointed at not getting his money's worth from it.

His favourite was the snake but it was quite tough and there was very little meat around the central vertebral column so he was left wanting more. It was like biting on a hard ear of corn to get the fleshy corn off the husk.

As we walked on, we learned another important lesson about finding unusual foods—the early worm catches the tourist. We had been so thrilled to spot that first cart that we purchased everything from a single vendor. Within half an hour, the entire street was filled with insect carts, ensuring that customers had more bargaining power. Many of these vendors were also calling out to us to taste their wares before making a purchase. We learned that we needed to wait so we could sample from many carts before making a choice henceforth.

'But do you know the best thing about eating bugs and spiders?' Vivek asked with a smile as we headed back to our hotel.

'Yes, yes. You've told me enough times that they're rich in protein and low on resources. And that they're the solution to the entire world's food problems,' I exclaimed, with the long-suffering air of someone who listens to this spiel multiple times a week.

'No,' said Vivek. 'The best thing about eating bugs and spiders is that you don't have to fight for the leg piece!'

Insect Cart, Khao San Road (Northeastern Thai Specialty)			
Item	*Mixed Insects*	*Fried Centipede and Fried Spider*	*Fried Watersnake*
Taste	★★	★	★★
Fear Factor	5	5	5
New Species	Grasshoppers, Silkworms, Bamboo Worms, Crickets, Beetles, Water bugs	Centipede, Spider	Snake
Price	฿200	฿100 and ฿200	฿500

Recipe: Bangkok Style Insects

Ingredients
Mixed bag of insects from a wholesale market in Bangkok
Oil of choice, preferably fresh
Salt and pepper to taste

Method
Heat the oil (feel free to use mustard seeds or jeera if you want
    to Indianize this)
Add insects and fry
Note: Insects are eaten whole, so there's no cutting or cleaning
    or removing of any parts involved in the cooking process
Enjoy!

To Market, to Market

Visiting a local market is one of the best ways to find authentic foods. Tourists typically do not visit these markets and even if they do, they stick to the sections with the food stalls which serve cooked dishes. Vivek likes walking through the fresh meat section of wholesale markets. On our second day in Bangkok, we headed to the city's largest wet market, Khlong Toei, so he could have a shot at finding species that we wouldn't see elsewhere.

Khlong Toei is a 'fresh' market, which offers low prices on seafood, raw meat and farm produce. While it is not too far from the city centre, it's tucked away into a corner of the Rama IV area and is not easily visible unless you know where you're going. It is easy to get to the market from the Khlong Toei MRT station. The market is at the intersection of Rama IV and Narong streets on the right side. These instructions seemed straightforward, so we took the subway. However, once we exited the station we couldn't figure out which way we needed to go. We also couldn't find someone who spoke English and getting directions was complex. We hadn't bothered to get a local SIM so we were navigating the old-school way. Soon we were able to locate a couple that told us which way to go. When we walked in the direction they pointed us at, we saw a footbridge and climbed it. The market is very clearly visible from the footbridge—there are rows and rows of tin roofs glinting in the sun. We quickly climbed down the bridge and came upon a row of stalls, which were on one of the outer edges of the market.

Most of the stalls in this area were food stalls where you could sample dishes. There were a few selling fresh produce and meat as well, but most of those were within the market. We decided to begin our market explorations by sampling the food. The first stall that looked interesting had a long grill on which many varieties of fish were cooking. Vivek was most curious about one particular kind of fish that was being steamed within a leaf. We practiced our sign language by asking the stall owner what type of fish this was, but she didn't speak any English and we couldn't get a response. Right next to the grill, the shop was also selling dried squid. This was available loose as well as packed in plastic bags. Based on Vivek's 'expert' interpretations, as well as this evidence, we garnered that she was serving squid steamed in a banana leaf.

Once Vivek sampled it he was able to confirm this wasn't squid, but also couldn't hazard a guess as to what fish it could be. The fish had no bones—it was like a processed fish product. Except that it was so fresh, it melted in the mouth. It was salty and mildly spiced with some herbs. From the looks of it, it appeared to have been steamed within the banana leaf in a method reminiscent of Malay cooking. Since we couldn't establish this as any particular species, Vivek decided to assume it was a fish he's already eaten. We went towards one of the entrances of the market.

Stall outside Khlong Toei Market, Rama IV Road (Northeastern Thai Specialty)	
Item	*Steamed fish wrapped in banana leaf*
Taste:	★★★★
Price:	฿20
Fear Factor:	2
New Species:	Unestablished

~

We entered into the fresh produce section. There was an odd, sickly sweet smell that I couldn't quite place. I'm used to meat markets smelling, but this was the first time I found a produce section smelling. Suddenly, I realized that we were walking by the durian, an innocuous-looking fruit that is so stinky it is banned from hotels and mass transit systems all over Southeast Asia. I wondered what would happen if I took one to the Airbnb. Would the hosts charge us extra for stinking up their apartment? Vivek's experiments were beginning to rub off on me. I also began to understand what a big deal it was for him to find and eat new unusual foods.

Before I could make up my mind on whether I should embark on an eating expedition of the vegetarian kind, we left the produce section and entered the meat section. The meat section of Khlong Toei is not for the squeamish. There is a lot of meat and unlike other markets where the meat is cut up into unidentifiable bits of flesh, the display is graphic. We saw fish of many shapes and sizes being thrown across from one side to the other. Some of them were still moving and jumping at passers-by. Clams, mussels and other shells were piled up in large heaps by the side of the fish.

Every other animal was being sold in a multitude of parts—you could pick pig ears, tongue, tail, hooves or any other part you desired by the kilogram. Birds were hanging upside down from the tops of the stalls and live frogs were being sold in plastic bags the way you get potatoes from a street-side vegetable vendor in India!

After a while, I started looking straight ahead to avoid looking directly into the eye of a dead chicken, or worse. Travelling can tell you a lot about the person you're with and my walk through that meat section was my way of telling Vivek just how far I was willing to go for him!

Khlong Toei: Wet markets are a must-visit

Soon, I started to get tired. Vivek, on the other hand, seemed determined to spend the entire day there. He was running this way and that trying to find something to cook and eat. Finally, I decided that it was time we added some sightseeing into the trip.

'Can we leave,' I asked, 'I really want to see at least one of the Buddha temples. They're beautiful and we shouldn't miss out on that experience.'

'We haven't seen the entire market yet,' said Vivek.

'Yes, but this market is ginormous. We will need to spend an entire day here if we want to see every corner. Can we at least move away from this section? I'm too worried to look sideways,' I said.

'Let's go out through that alley near the corner,' he said. 'I have an intuition that there's something there.'

I agreed and we walked towards the alley.

'Oh my God! They have rats! I can cook them in the Airbnb,' said Vivek.

I turned and saw rows of dead rats displayed along the aisle. They were large, fat and had their mouths open. I am not very squeamish about most of the weird foods that Vivek eats but these rats looked disgusting. The thought of him cooking these at the Airbnb where I'd have to face them closely was off-putting.

'If you're bringing a dead rat back into that Airbnb, you can live there by yourself,' I retorted.

For some reason, he didn't push very hard. I chose to believe that he decided to skip eating a rat just for me. I suspect, however, that the rats were as raw as the chickens I'd spotted earlier and he didn't want the fuss of cleaning and cutting it, especially since the only knife we'd spotted at the Airbnb was a butter knife. Or maybe, this wasn't about the rats. Maybe, there was more to that alley.

A little way ahead, a lady was selling what looked like a heap of puffed rice. It turned out to be a heap of ant eggs. The eggs were relatively large, about 7–8 mm in size. The outer skin was wet and squishy. I couldn't believe that a tiny ant would have such large eggs.

'These are ant eggs from red weaver ants,' Vivek clarified. 'They are much larger than the ants at home. These ants walk around in the jungle with serious business!'

As he said this, I realized that a mound of darkish wasp-like insects displayed next to the eggs were the ants in question. I marvelled at their size as he went on to tell me more about them. Wild ants make nests on trees in the jungles. The locals catch them by shaking the nests in such a way that the eggs fall into a basket that's placed underneath to collect them. The gatherer of ant eggs has a job rivalling that of beekeepers—as he shakes the nests, he gets bitten by the angry ants. These ants are a very popular snack in Thailand and Laos and a major source of protein.[11]

Just as I was about to ask how he was such a fount of wisdom on all things ant-related, he confessed he had come to Khlong Toei with the express purpose of finding these very eggs. He couldn't believe that our persistent yet haphazard wandering had somehow led us right to it.

'I told you my intuition with finding new species is very good,' he said. 'This market is so large that our chances of finding this particular seller were minimal.'

We went up to the vendor to figure out the price of the eggs. We already knew that English wasn't going to work, so Vivek jumped directly into sign language. He pointed at the eggs, raised one finger (to signify one kilogram) and drew a question mark in the air. The woman very confidently raised six fingers.

'Wow! It's only ฿6! That's so awesome. Now, let me try bargaining,' he said. With a lot of hand waving and head shaking, he was able to bring it down to ฿5 (the lady had shown him five fingers and a thumbs-up on her other hand). She weighed everything and handed us a plastic bag filled with the eggs. We handed over the ฿5 and she looked perplexed. She began shaking her head and pointing at her wallet which is when we realized we'd missed something. There was more hand waving and we tried a few words like five, kilo and so on.

Finally, she marched up to the neighbouring stall and brought back a calculator. She typed '500' on it and that's when the penny dropped. She was selling one kilogram of ant eggs for ฿500. Vivek decided that one kilogram of ant eggs was too much and after ten more minutes of bargaining, he purchased 250 gm of ant eggs and another 250 gm combo of ant eggs with ants. We left the market and I tossed the plastic cover of our purchases into my backpack.

Later that night, we decided to cook the ant eggs. The first thing we discovered was that the book I was carrying in the backpack had squashed the ant eggs, so they were now mushy. The kitchen had very few seasoning ingredients so we decided to stir-fry the eggs in butter and add a splash of soy sauce for taste. The end result was the tastiest egg bhurji we've ever tried. It was tangy, as though we had squeezed lemon on it. Vivek's theory, which I later discovered is true, is that the ants eat mango leaves in the forest, which results in this lemony taste. He had his bhurji with some of the ants and liked the crunch that they added to the dish. If you prefer your eggs insect-free, like I do, you should stay away from the combo bag of eggs and ants.

Vivek almost always prioritizes meat over eggs, but in this case, he maintains that this bhurji is one of the tastiest of all the weird food he's eaten. I think some credit should go to me for my recipe and for the pre-squashing of the eggs.

Khlong Toei Market, Rama IV Road, Khlong Toei (North-Eastern Thai Specialty)	
Item	*Ant Egg Bhurji, with some topping of ants*
Taste	★★★★★
Price	฿250
Fear Factor	5
New Species	Ant Eggs, Weaver Ants

Recipe: Ant Egg Bhurji

Ingredients
250 gm combo bag of giant ant eggs with a sprinkling of
     weaver ants
Butter
Soy Sauce
A bookworm spouse who pre-squashes the egg with a book
Google Translate app in offline mode for negotiations

Method
Pour some butter on a pan
Add the ant-egg combo and stir-fry in the butter for about
     2–3 minutes
Add soy sauce (to taste)
Serve with local beer (Chang or Singha)
Enjoy!

House of Birds

After our trip to Khlong Toei, we went to the Wat Pho and Wat Arun temples. While the main objective of our trip was to sample Thai cuisine, it seemed wrong to leave Bangkok without seeing a single Buddha. So we took a break from eating to see these two temples and then head out to Yaowarat Road, Bangkok's Chinatown area.

Yaowarat Road looks innocuous during the day but serves as a food lover's paradise after dark. There are restaurants serving authentic Chinese food, as well as street vendors who set up shop only at night. Vivek strongly believes that all good things can be found in Chinatown and insists on visiting it everywhere we go. Maybe the fascination with Chinatown will finally end when we visit China.

~

At Wat Pho, the temple of the reclining Buddha, you will find a large, gold statue of Buddha in a reclining posture. The feet alone are five metres in length and lined with pearls. Just standing in front of that statue is a meditative experience since a single look doesn't allow you to see the statue in its entirety. You end up seeing it in parts as you move around the sanctum. As I stood in front of the massive feet, I felt like I was a tiny, insignificant speck in the overall scheme of the universe. We spent a couple of hours going around the complex. By the time we left the temple, it was well past noon. As we walked outside the temple complex, we found a small cafe advertising Boat Noodles.

'Boat Noodles' originated in the Central Thai region, on the Chao Phraya River which runs through Bangkok. Vendors on a canoe would prepare the steaming hot noodles while they navigated through the city's extensive waterways. These vendors would paddle up to a bridge where people were congregating and serve them noodles from the boat.[12] Boat noodles are served in a deep, small bowl because vendors would have to serve the noodles and also handle money so this format worked to ensure the bowl wasn't dropped into the canal. Customers sit on the bridge and eat the noodles. We were very excited to discover boat noodles in this area, even though it wasn't on the river.

Boat Noodles

The cafe had two varieties of the boat noodles—one with the traditional beef and the other with pork, which Vivek tried. The traditional base for boat noodles is a stock that is made of herbs and spices, with a sweet and sour taste. The ingredients in the broth include galangal, ginger lemongrass, kaffir lime leaves, pepper, cinnamon, coriander, pickled bean curd and coagulated blood from the protein that is used. The blood adds thickness to the broth. Vivek was very conflicted about eating this because of the blood—while he was open to eating all kinds of species, blood was gory. When he broke through the mental barrier and ordered it, he realized that coagulated blood doesn't really look bloody and instead adds a dusty look to the soup. The cafe served the pork version with rice noodles, morning glory, bean sprouts and barbecued pork.

While we stumbled upon the dish in the Banglamphu area, the best place to sample boat noodles is at the street-side vendors and restaurants near the Victory Monument in the Ratchathewi district.

Unnamed Café, Banglamphu (Central Thai Specialty)	
Item	*Boat Noodles with Pork*
Taste	★★★★
Price	฿15
Fear Factor	4
New Species	Coagulated Blood

~

Our next stop was across the river—the Wat Arun, or the temple of dawn. It is named after the Indian God Aruna, the God of dawn. Since the temple is on the banks of the Chao Phraya River, it is a great place to see the sunset. The temple complex is large and beautiful. The design of Wat Arun is very different from that of other temples in Bangkok, as it includes a massive 'prang' or tower that is built in the Khmer architectural style. Standing tall at eighty metres, this is the highest tower in Thailand.[13] Since the temple is on the banks of the river, it also stands to reason that there's some really good seafood being sold right outside the temple complex.

Once we were done looking around the temple, we walked out into the larger complex to find something to eat. In addition to the stalls selling souvenirs and memorabilia, there are food stalls. We found a vendor selling grilled squid. While this was a street-side stall, the vendors put a lot of effort into their plating. The squid was served in the centre of a plastic plate, with dipping sauces on the side and topped with a purple flower to accentuate the dish. Vivek got rid of the flower and got down to the business of devouring the squid in minutes. Squids are chewy and firm, with a mild but distinct taste that mimics the sea. This one was well cooked, ensuring that it maintained the balance of cooking with the taste and texture. It came with two kinds of sauces, sweet and spicy. The combination of the two packed just the right punch for the dish. Once he was done with this appetizer, he was all set to head to Chinatown for the main course.

Grilled squid

Street-Side Vendor, Wat Arun complex (Central Thai Specialty)	
Item	*Grilled Squid*
Taste	★★★★
Price	฿50
Fear Factor	2
New Species	Squid

~

Our next stop was Yaowarat Road where the primary objective was to find 'Bird's Nest Soup', a translucent soup made from a bird's nest. The bird in question is the swiftlet, which lives in caves in Southeast Asia. The swiftlet takes thirty days to make its nest using saliva instead of twigs. The dried saliva is one of the weirdest ingredients found in a food item. The demand for this dish is so high in places like Hong Kong that it's one of the most expensive dishes there.[14] Thankfully, this was not the case in Bangkok. There are two industries at work to supply this dish—one to collect the birds' nests from the wild and the second to tame the birds so there's a steady supply of birds' nests for consumption.

There are many restaurants in Chinatown that serve Bird's Nest Soup and are quite affordable, but we had already decided that we would visit Hua Seng Hong, which was highly recommended. It's also known to be authentic, a key requirement for a dish that's spurred an entire industry to manufacture fake bird's nest edible replicas.

Yaowarat Road is not easily accessible by the MRT, so we took a cab to the entrance. We looked for Hua Seng Hong on foot. It was hard to spot at first as the road around it was under construction. However, we were soon able to spot the giant red signboard with a mascot of a chef serving food in a wok. Despite the construction and debris on the road outside, we could see a steady stream of patrons entering the restaurant, further strengthening our belief that this would be the best place to eat in Chinatown.

We were able to get a table right away. Vivek placed an order for Bird's Nest Soup. The soup was thick, with soft pieces of the bird's nest. It looked like the translucent sweet corn soup, with pieces floating around it that was akin to the mango pulp in a milkshake. The thickness of the soup comes from corn starch that's added into the stock. It's gelatinous when mixed with water. Contrary to what you'd expect when you think of eating saliva, the soup tasted really good.

It is said that the taste depends on the origins of the bird and what it eats, so we had found one that had definitely eaten the right things.

Bird's Nest Soup

Hua Seng Hong also served oyster omelette, which is another popular Thai dish. The oyster omelette looked a lot like *shakshuka*, the Middle Eastern poached egg dish with spicy tomato sauce. In this case, the shakshuka-like skillet was topped with oysters that were well steamed. It came with a side of spicy chilli sauce and some lemon juice to add an extra kick. Compared to most other Thai dishes, this one is greasy because it's deep fried to make it crispy. Nevertheless, this is one of the best street foods that you will find in Bangkok.

Oyster omelette

While Vivek sampled the soup and the omelette, I started using the restaurant's Wi-Fi to see what else we could eat and discovered that Yaowarat was also the area to try out Yaowarat Toasted Bread, a highly recommended street vendor who sells toast.

Hua Seng Hong, 371–373 Yaowrat Road (Central Thai Specialty)		
Item	*Bird's Nest Soup*	*Oyster Omelette*
Taste	★★★★	★★★★
Price	฿500	฿180
Fear Factor	4 (if you're squeamish about birds' saliva)	2
New Species	Bird's Nest	Oysters

~

We left Hua Seng Hong and I started walking in circles to find the toast shop. All directions say that it can be spotted directly outside the Government Savings Bank, but I found it really hard to locate the bank. As we were wandering around trying to find the bank, I saw a group of teenagers eating something that looked exactly like the toast. So, I accosted them and asked them for directions. Unlike Vivek who makes friends with people to find out where to eat, I looked like a demented explorer. The teenagers gave me directions so I would go away and let them eat their toast in peace. It turned out to be a good thing that I harassed them though—what I'd thought was a large procession and studiously avoided all evening turned out to be the crowds making their way to Yaowarat Toasted Bread!

We believe that any place that is patronized by locals is likely to be good and by that logic, this toast shop was clearly going to be fantastic. In addition to the crowd we'd joined, there was a queue spilling onto the road near the stall. I quickly realized that waiting in line wasn't the way to get served. People walk up to the stall, write out an order and their name on a piece of paper and drop it into a bucket. They then wait in the queue while the staff picks up the order from the bucket, makes it and yells out the name and number.

The toast comes with a choice of various toppings—chocolate, peanut, marmalade, milk, pineapple, strawberry, sugar, egg custard (*kaya*) and chilli. You can also opt for the buns to be crispy or crispy and soft. I picked the kaya topping on a crispy bun on the recommendation of one of the staff at the stall. I also got a chocolate bun and then went to wait in the queue.

Searching for the toast on Yaowarat Road

After about twenty minutes, my name was called out. The toast was fabulous and I regretted not buying more. To enjoy this fabulous, melt-in-your-mouth toast, ask one of the locals on Yaowarat Road to help you locate it or just follow the crowds. Neither the signboard on the stall nor the one for the Government Savings Bank is written in English, though the bank features a distinctive bright pink board.

As we went back, Vivek asked, 'Do you know that Bird's Nest Soup is one of the most expensive foods on the planet? They cost between $2000–$10,000 a kilo.'

'What! That's Rs 6 lakhs!' I exclaimed.

'Yes, the prices have skyrocketed for bird housing as well,' he grinned.

20 THB 452, Yaowarat Road (Central Thai Specialty)	
Item	*Kaya Toast and Chocolate Toast on Crispy Buns*
Taste	★★★★★
Price	฿20
Fear Factor	1
New Species	None

What Floats Our Boat

Floating markets originated in times where water transportation was key to daily life in Thailand. At the time, markets were set up on boats in the canals and waterways in the city.[15] Today, there's no need for floating markets, but these markets continue to be massive tourist attractions. There are a few that are frequented by locals. Typical tour itineraries in Bangkok will take you to floating markets that are very close to the city. We discovered that Taling Chan Floating Market is very popular with the locals. It was highly recommended as being one of the best places in Bangkok to try fresh seafood. Unlike some of the other floating markets that sell everything from trinkets and souvenirs to produce and cooked food, Taling Chan is primarily a food market.

While it was easy to find out that Taling Chan was the market to visit, it was much harder to get directions to reach there. It's a little ways away from the city so there isn't a subway stop nearby. There was a complicated bus route, so we decided to take a cab instead. Vivek downloaded the directions to Taling Chan and ensured that he had screenshots of the name and location written down in Thai so we could show it to our cab driver. We flagged a cab and showed him the screenshots. The cab driver seemed to understand exactly where we wanted to go. He displayed his confidence by repeating 'Taling Chan Market' and showing us two thumbs up. We climbed in and each began reading our respective books. Half an hour later, the cab halted and the driver said, 'Market.'

We got out of the cab and realized that we couldn't see any water nearby. There were a lot of stalls clustered together. The stalls were selling clothes, sunglasses and other knickknacks. We looked around for the pier, but we couldn't see any food stalls. Suddenly, I spotted a large sign saying 'Chatuchak Market'. That's when I realized that the driver had put together the words 'tourist' and 'market' to determine that we were headed to the Chatuchak Weekend Market. Not only did he not know English, but he also couldn't read the Thai directions we had shown him. While we planned to head to Chatuchak later in the day, it was quite clear that all tourists head to Chatuchak first thing on a Saturday morning and this cab driver assumed we would do the same. However, our priority was the fresh food at Taling Chan. We wanted to go there and eat before we shopped. So, we hailed another cab to take us back there. This time around, we double and triple checked that the cab driver knew exactly where we were headed, so we didn't accidentally end up being dropped off at a different gate of Chatuchak Market!

The entrance is flanked by stalls selling plants. Further down, there are food stalls on either side leading up to a large boat. The food stalls were selling snacks on sticks, grilled snacks, quail eggs and desserts, including the very popular Thai dessert, mango sticky rice. I made a note to come back for it later.

The walkway from the entrance leads to a giant boat filled with tables where you can sit and eat. The centre of the boat is covered and the bow and stern areas have open-air tables. The food is sold from smaller boats on either side of the giant boat. These smaller boats also serve as barbecue kitchen areas. Vendors were grilling fish and clams on the smaller boats.

Taling Chan vendors all have similar menus. However, every vendor places their menu on the tables. That way, people can choose to buy all the dishes from a single vendor, or sample different dishes across vendors. The servers take your order and then bring the food from the floating boats on the side of the deck. We took a walk to see which vendor's food looked the most appetizing and then picked a spot on the table by that vendor.

Taling Chan Floating Market: A unique experience

Once we found the perfect spot, Vivek opted to try the fresh clams, as well as a grilled tilapia main course. I had the Thai papaya salad and we both had Thai iced tea to drink. The papaya salad was fresh, light and well flavoured with the spicy-sweet peanut sauce. The iced tea was the most underwhelming part of the meal—it was cloyingly sweet and didn't have the balance of flavours that we'd come to expect from our meals in Bangkok.

'Eating fish closest to the source is the best! I'm sure they caught this fish earlier today,' said Vivek. 'It tastes so fresh and so good!'

He savoured every bite of the large tilapia and picked at it to ensure none of it went waste. Tilapia is a neutral-flavoured fish which takes on the flavour of the sauce. In this case, it had a smokiness from the grill mixed with the smell of the water, the freshness of the fish and the barbecue sauce.

The fresh clams were steamed and served with some sauce. Clams have a similar, distinct taste of snails and other bivalves, of the earthiness in water. These clams were slightly salty and chewy. Vivek got busy pulling the clams apart. It reminded me of splitting open the whole peanuts sold on the beach. Sometimes the shell wouldn't come apart easily. At such times, he used a fork to pull out the bean-shaped meat and relished it. When I asked him which of the two he preferred, he was hard-pressed to pick a favourite because they were both fresh and extremely well cooked.

There's something about eating on a platform on the water—it gives you the chance to eat out in the open and in this case you also watch your food being prepared live. The closest comparison is eating at a beach shack where you can look out onto the ocean while you eat. But over there, you're still on land. Over here, you also feel a mild movement from the water while you're sitting. We sat there for a couple of hours and if it weren't for the fact that we were quite stuffed, we would've ordered more.

Grilled tilapia and steamed clams: Bought off a boat

Taling Chan Floating Market, 300 Soi Chak Phra 17 (Southern Thai Specialty)			
Item	*Thai Papaya Salad*	*Grilled Tilapia*	*Steamed Clams*
Taste	★★★	★★★★	★★★
Price	฿50–60	฿170	฿100
Fear Factor	1	1	3
New Species	None	None	Clams

~

On our way out of Taling Chan, I made sure to stop at the stall selling mango sticky rice. The sticky rice is accompanied with a sauce made of tapioca starch, coconut milk, sugar and salt, topped with mangoes. I ate many plates of mango sticky rice after this one and none of them matched up. The mangoes were fresh, juicy and really sweet. The blandness of the rice cut the sweetness of the mango and coconut milk combination perfectly, ensuring that the dessert wasn't overly sweet.

As I ate it, I told myself that I'd start making the same at home during mango season. Or, I could just walk around in Southeast Asia in April during mango season and have it served to me on a platter!

Walkway, Taling Chan Floating Market, 300 Soi Chak Phra 17 (Northern Thai Specialty)	
Item	*Mango Sticky Rice*
Taste	★★★★★
Price	฿20
Fear Factor	1
New Species	None

~

From Taling Chan, we headed out to Chatuchak Market. We weren't expecting to find a new dish here since we were there to shop. However, after a few hours of walking in the sun, I went to find something to drink. Right next to the stall selling the strawberry ice was a stall selling squid eggs. Even though Vivek had claimed he was stuffed barely an hour ago at the Floating Market, he said that the walking around had already helped him get some space to try these out.

It was the first time he had ever come across squid eggs. He had tried squid earlier so he wondered why he hadn't found squid eggs before. The market offered squid eggs cooked two ways—deep-fried and pan-fried. Vivek tried the pan-fried version so that he wasn't distracted from the taste of the eggs by the taste of the batter it's deep-fried in.

Squid eggs

Each egg tasted like a squid packed into an egg, bringing out the flavour of squid more sharply. He also found the eggs to be tastier than the squid since the taste was so concentrated.

After this meal, Vivek decided to add a new branch to the food chart, eggs.

Street Vendor, Chatuchak Market, Kamphaeng Phet 3 Rd, Khwaeng Lat Yao, Khet Chatuchak (Southern Thai Specialty)	
Item	*Squid Eggs*
Taste	★★★★
Price	฿50
Fear Factor	3
New Species	Squid Eggs

~

That night, we went to the mall near the 9 MRT Station for dinner because we were tired. As we approached the mall, we realized that the streets outside were filled with food stalls. Vendors were busy grilling various types of meat. Vivek quickly sampled barbecued crab, chicken and prawns. Once he was done with these appetizers, we headed to the food court for our main course.

'Are you still hungry?' I asked him.

'Of course,' he said. 'When I eat, the different animals make space for each other in my stomach!'

I didn't want to dignify that mental image with a response, so I busied myself with buying myself a plate of pad thai and finding a table. Vivek wandered around to see if he could find a new species. Contrary to my expectations, he discovered a restaurant where the menu looked like 'a textbook of a pig's anatomy'. He came back with a pig's foot curry and rice meal.

He seemed to be struggling to eat it even though he was enthusiastic about the dish. When I asked him why he didn't get something else, he said that it seemed stinky to him, but not to the locals so it was just a case of opening up his mind to it. He also said it had a strong aftertaste.

I realized that it's very important to always keep your eyes peeled if you're interested in trying unusual foods. While I wouldn't have expected to find something new at a food court, I'd forgotten that a mall in Bangkok would have local favourites that would be unusual foods for those of us from elsewhere.

We chose Bangkok so we could try as many Thai cuisines as possible. We were successful in trying out dishes from different regions in Thailand, though the insects weren't really 'cooked' in any style. On our next trip, we plan to head to the

North and North-eastern parts of the country to sample the
local styles of cooking unusual foods.

Food Court, Central Plaza, Grand Rama IX, 9 9 Ratchadaphisek Rd, Khwaeng Huai Khwang, Khet Huai Khwang (Central Thai Specialty)	
Item	*Pigs' Foot Curry with Rice*
Taste	★★
Price	฿100
Fear Factor	4
New Species	Pigs' Foot

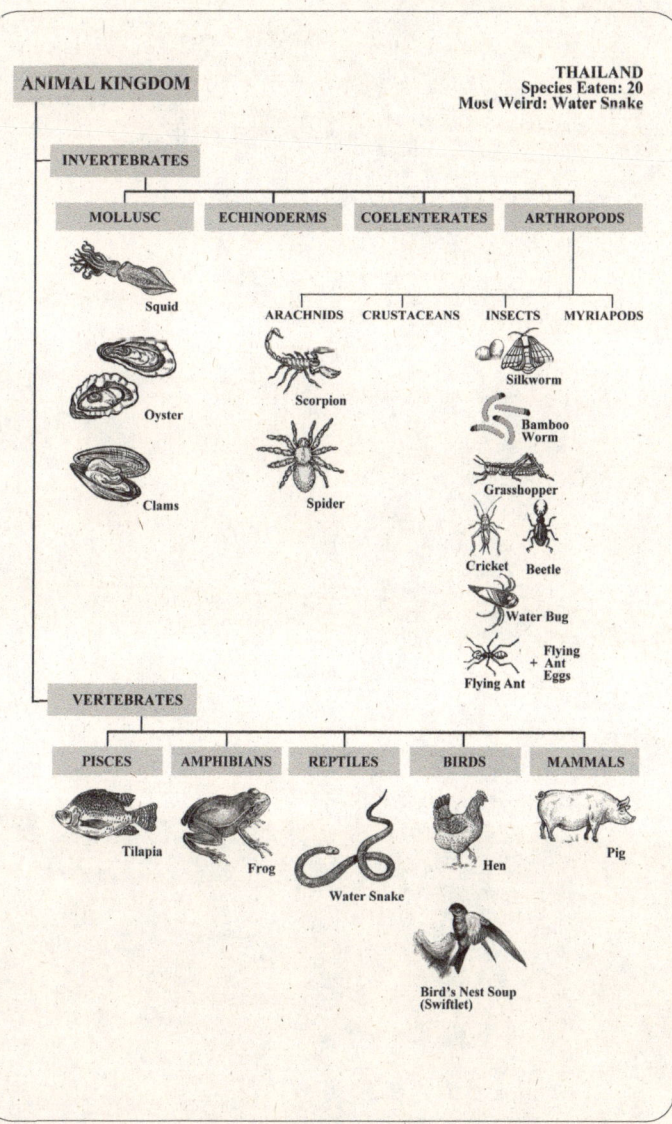

ANIMAL KINGDOM

INVERTEBRATES

MOLLUSC   **ECHINODERMS**   **COELENTERATES**   **ARTHROPODS**

Squid

ARACHNIDS   **CRUSTACEANS**   **INSECTS**   **MYRIAPODS**

Oyster

Silkworm

Scorpion

Bamboo Worm

Clams

Grasshopper

Spider

Cricket   Beetle

Water Bug

Flying Ant   + Flying Ant Eggs

VERTEBRATES

PISCES   **AMPHIBIANS**   **REPTILES**   **BIRDS**   **MAMMALS**

Tilapia

Frog

Hen

Pig

Water Snake

Bird's Nest Soup (Swiftlet)

AUSTRALIA

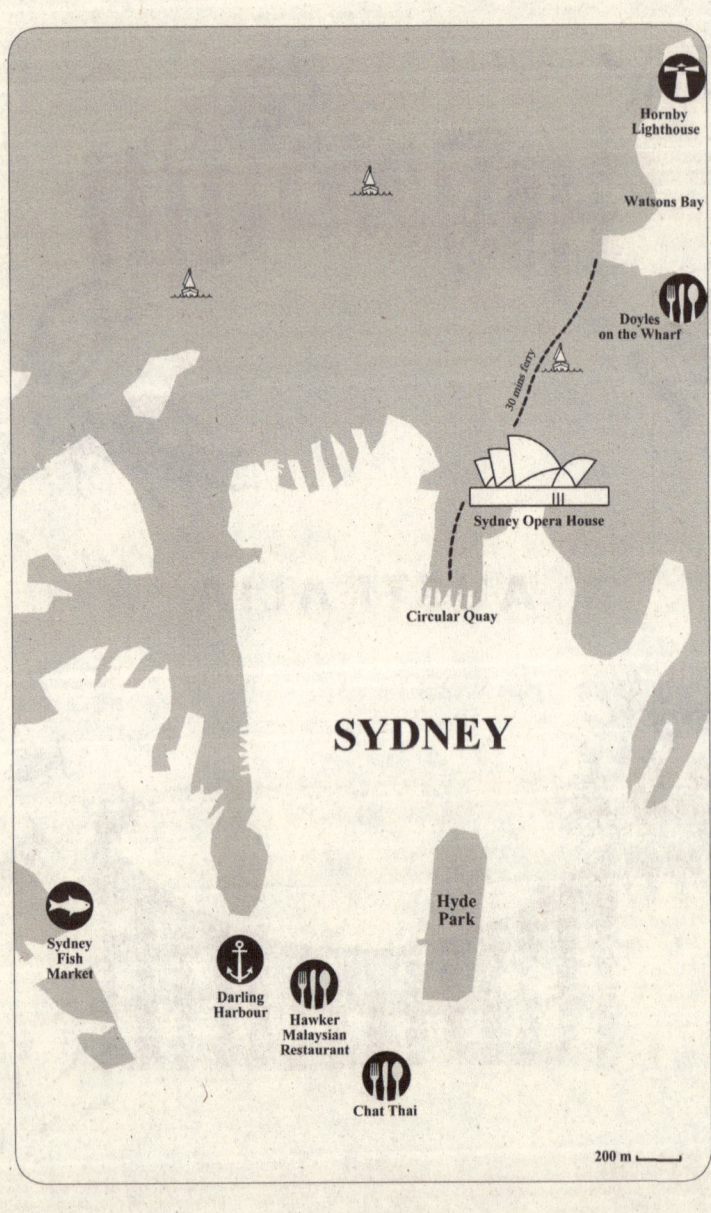

Hornby
Lighthouse

Watsons Bay

Doyles
on the Wharf

30 min ferry

Sydney Opera House

Circular Quay

SYDNEY

Hyde
Park

Sydney
Fish
Market

Darling
Harbour

Hawker
Malaysian
Restaurant

Chat Thai

200 m

Many of the prettiest photographs that I've seen are often from Australia. The blues of the Great Barrier Reef, the reds and browns of the outback, the varied hues of greens in the tropical rainforests, the yellows of the lights along the Sydney Harbour, are all lit up in shades of technicolour that you would rarely have ever experienced elsewhere. The laidback nature of the locals and the good food also combine to make it a great destination for a vacation.

Australian cuisine showcases the colonial British influences with dishes like fish and chips, roast dinners and meat pies. Meat is a core component of Australian cuisine and nothing says Australia like a good outdoorsy barbecue, or 'barbie', does. Before the arrival of the Europeans, however, indigenous Australians survived off the local flora and fauna. Therefore, hunting of emus, kangaroos and wallabies was common. Other foods consumed included Bogong moths, witchetty grubs, lizards and snakes. Bush berries, fruits and honey are also widely used in the local cuisine.

Australia is the third largest fishing zone in the world, resulting in some of the best and freshest seafood in the world being available here. Australian cuisine features local seafood like southern Bluefin tuna, King George whiting, Moreton Bay bug, mud crab, dhufish and yabby. Australia is also the largest producer of abalone and rock lobster.

We spent two weeks in Australia in 2016, where we travelled to Sydney, Melbourne, Cairns and the Great Barrier Reef and Tasmania. We were able to experiment with many local foods, as well as some new varieties from the cuisines of other countries.

Spice in Disguise

The first thing that hit me when we got out of Sydney airport was just how bright it is. I knew that the sun in Australia would be much brighter because of the giant hole in the Ozone, but I hadn't expected to feel it so strongly. The second thing that hit me was how tired I was. Sydney is a long flight away from Bangalore and I was longing for a nap. But naps are the biggest enemies of jetlag. Thankfully, it turned out that Shreyas, the friend we were staying with, was already prepared with a daylong trip that he termed a jetlag killer.

That's how we found ourselves on a ferry ride to Watson's Bay, which houses Macquarie Lighthouse, Australia's oldest functional lighthouse.[16] There's a short climb that takes you to the lighthouse and if you go at the right time, you can watch a gorgeous sunset.

We pulled up right by the bay in our water taxi. This part of the beach had a line of restaurants. Of the restaurants on this strip, 'Doyle's Fisherman Wharf' appeared to have the best views of the bay. Shreyas told us this restaurant came highly recommended, so we decided to have lunch there. Vivek was hoping they served John Dory fish, a local specialty. John Dory is a fish commonly found in the waters by Sydney Harbour and is one the Australians call their own.

It's finely grained, meaty and decadent, a perfect pairing to a night spent partying.

We found ourselves a good table by the window so we could look out onto the beach while we ate. Vivek was thrilled to find that the restaurant did indeed serve the John Dory, so we immediately ordered a plate of that. We also got some salad and garlic bread.

John Dory on the beach

The pan-fried John Dory had a firm, flaky texture and a mild, slightly sweet flavour. It was ironic how a fish that goes out of its way to look unappetizing could be so delicious. The John Dory is flat, bony and adorned with lethal spikes. It also has a large black spot on the side that looks a little like an eye. Predators often mistake this to be the real eyes and attack its midsection, giving it a chance to escape. It's not an easy fish to find and its closest substitutes are probably tilapia, sole and Dover fish. But nothing really beats the original John Dory.

Roasted squab at International District—fully reconstructed

Balut—half egg, half bird, complete courage

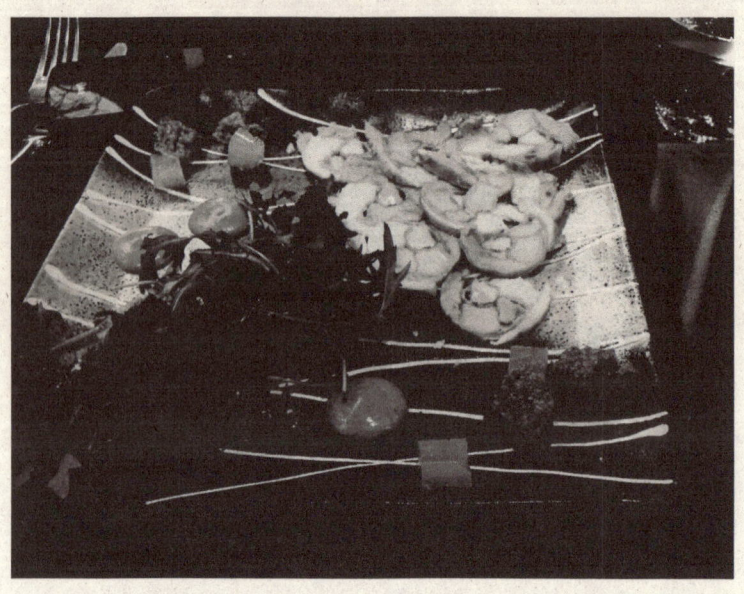

Smoked python at Archipelago, London. Vivek swallowed it whole.

Horse steak at Luxembourg City. You need horsepower to finish it.

Insect cart at Khao San Road, Bangkok—test your fears here

Ant eggs by the kilo at Khlong Toei, Bangkok. Perfect for egg bhurji!

Grilled seafood cart at Wat Arun, Bangkok

Fish market at Sydney, Australia

Stingray at Hawker Malaysian, Sydney

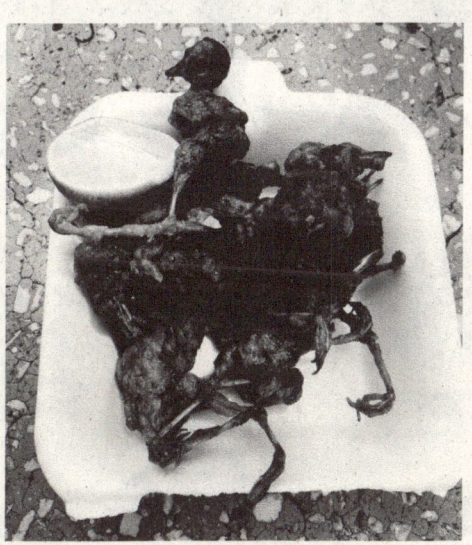

Fried sparrows at Psar Chaa Market, Siem Reap

Roasted Frogs, Khmer Taste, Siem Reap—a leap of taste

Razor clams and sea snail at Ben Thanh Market, Ho Chi Minh City

Pick your seafood at Phu Quoc Night Market

Sea urchin at Phu Quoc Night Market, Phu Quoc

Moreton Bay bug at East Coast Road Food Centre, Singapore

Puffer fish at Guenpin Fugu, Singapore—the biggest dare

As Vivek put it, 'I think this is a special meal. This beach is so beautiful and the wind smells so clean. I feel reenergized just by sitting here and eating.'

'What's so special about the fish?' I asked.

'Actually, I like how the John Dory looks, like an alien creature from *The Hitchhiker's Guide to the Galaxy* with a strange mohawk,' he replied.

Doyle's Fisherman's Wharf, Watsons Bay	
Item	*Pan-fried John Dory*
Taste	★★★★
Price	AUD20
Fear Factor	2
New Species	John Dory

~

The next day we went to the Opera House and walked around Darling Harbour and the Quay. After a full day of sightseeing, we went out for dinner to Chat Thai, a Thai restaurant that Shreyas recommended. Although we prefer local food when we travel, Chat Thai was in Sydney's Chinatown and, as you well know, we love exploring Chinatowns. I was excited at being able to eat some good Thai papaya salad and secretly hoping that Chat Thai had managed to source fresh mangoes so they could serve mango sticky rice for dessert. I was conveniently ignoring the fact that this was October. I reasoned that if people in Cairns were brewing mango wine, then we had a shot at finding fresh mangoes in Sydney.

The restaurant was tucked away into a corner. The walls were adorned with images of food carts, restaurants and bowls giving the impression that one had stepped off the streets of

Sydney onto a street in Bangkok. The menu reiterated that
the food was authentic Thai street cuisine. The restaurant had
two levels. We went up to the second level and got a table
near the staircase. This gave us a great view of the Thai street
illustrations along the stairway as well as those on the walls. As
I pointed out things I recognized from Bangkok, Vivek got
busy with the menu.

'I think I will have the Thai papaya salad today, too,' he says.

'Does this mean that we can share?' I asked hopefully.

'Of course not! Not unless you want to eat just the
papaya bits from mine, because I'm ordering the version with
fermented fish!'

I was no longer surprised. My foodie spouse had
immediately zeroed in onto the fact that Chat Thai had a
fermented fish version of the salad, proving that he isn't
kidding when he says he looks at menus and sees species, not
dishes. Shreyas and I opted for non-fermented food, the Thai
chicken curry and pad thai.

Pia ra, or fermented fish, is a key ingredient in North-
eastern Thai cuisine and is said to have originated in the
Mekong basin. It is prepared by fermenting fish with rice
bran or roasted rice powder and salt and fermented in a closed
container for at least six months. Dishes that use fermented fish
have a very strong smell.

The salad looked delicious, smell notwithstanding. The
vegetables were super fresh and there was a generous smattering
of peanuts and peanut sauce. Vivek promptly took a heaping
forkful. He barely put the spoon in his mouth when he had a
coughing fit.

'What happened? Does the fish taste really bad?' I asked.

'No,' he choked out, as tears began to roll down his eyes.
'This is super spicy.'

'Did she ask you to give her a spice level on a scale of 1–5?'
I ask, knowing that many Thai restaurants do this because not
everyone can handle some of the potent Thai chillies. I've
learnt this the hard way and only ask for a Thai 2. For the
spice lovers out there, I know that this is like asking for a dish
off the children's menu, but at least I haven't ever looked as
red-faced and teary-eyed as Vivek did. He could barely get the
words out to reply.

'She didn't. But even if she asked, I would've said 5
because I can handle any spice,' he exclaimed.

I raised my eyebrows as he promptly continued to defend
his ability to eat spicy food.

'This isn't a spice. The dish is like ingesting chemicals.
And it's slowly dissolving the walls of my stomach.'

'I think there's visible proof that you may not be able to
handle a Thai 5,' I said, quietly.

But Vivek isn't one to give in, especially when it comes to
food. He soldiered on as Shreyas and I bet on whether smoke
would emanate from his ears. After a few bites, he realized that
eating more of the salad would ensure he wouldn't be eating at
all for the rest of the trip. And so, he did what any sane non-
vegetarian foodie would do. He isolated all the fish and ate it
all. Not one bite of fish was wasted, though he did collect a
mountain of papaya, peanuts and vegetables. He claimed his
dish was less spicy that way, but his voice lacked the usual
baritone.

Thankfully for him, the main course turned out to be
normally spiced and he was able to use it to douse his burning
tongue. The Thai chicken curry was as good as any in Thailand
and the jasmine rice was fluffed to perfection. The pad thai was
also seasoned well and had a generous helping of peanuts that
were enough to convince me that I had made the right choice.

I later asked Vivek if that salad was the spiciest thing he's ever eaten.

'Yes,' he said. 'The only thing which came close was the turtle soup I had in Portland.'

'You mean the soup you sneaked off to eat at that restaurant, The Parish, while my parents and I were down the road at Powell's bookstore? Didn't that upset your stomach? I remember my mother decided that non-vegetarian food doesn't agree with you,' I laughed.

'Yes, it did give me a stomach ache and that's only because of how spicy it was. *Woh turtle kaafi tez tha!*'*

Chat Thai, 20 Campbell Street, Haymarket			
Item	Som Dtum Bpu Bpla La (Papaya salad with fermented fish)	Gaeang Keaw Gai (Green Chicken Curry)	Pad Thai
Taste	★★	★★★★★	★★★★
Price	AUD13	AUD5	AUD12
Fear Factor	5	1	1
New Species	Fermented Fish	None	None

---

* That turtle was really spicy

The Young Man and the Seafood

The Sydney fish market was established in the year 1966 and is next to one of the largest working fishing ports in the world, on Blackwattle Bay in Pyrmont, about 2 km west of the central business district.[17] The market was on our list of places to visit, but we didn't realize just how close we were to it. Shreyas happened to live down the road from the market, making it one of our first stops on a Monday morning.

We took a walk down to the pier near the market. On one side were the loading docks, against which many boats lined up. On the other side, was the large wholesale fish market. The pathway just outside the market had seagulls flocking about to see if they could find an errant fish lying on the roadside to eat. Inside, the market was enormous with multiple stalls, supermarkets and stores. At the back of the market was a food court where vendors were cooking the fresh catch from the market. There were dining areas within the food court and outside by the pier. We started by exploring the stalls and supermarkets inside the fish market.

Once we stepped inside, we were struck by how large it was. It looked like a never-ending warehouse. Most of the market was focused on fresh and frozen seafood sales and at the back was a large food court for freshly prepared seafood. We walked into one of the large shops, which looked like a giant supermarket. Instead of aisles, the central area of this shop had a clean, brightly lit counter displaying an enormous variety of fish, shellfish and other seafood in glass cases. Around the edges were large aquariums with live oysters, scallops, abalone, lobsters, crabs and sea cucumbers. It was well organized with the catch segregated by species. There was a mindboggling variety of seafood—oysters, tuna, barramundi, salmon and even octopi. Everything was laid out neatly and ordered by size. Vivek exclaimed in delight when he saw the more exotic local species like abalone, sea cucumber and Moreton Bay bugs.

All the walking around in the market made us hungry, so we went to the food court to start sampling the catch. Vivek was thrilled to see that the food court also served abalone. Abalone is a type of univalve marine snail. It has a protective shell on one side and a row of pores for respiration. Within the tank, we could see the hair-like tentacles coming out from all sides of the shell. While we've spotted it in Southeast Asia, it's always been expensive and priced as high as AUD50–70 because of its rarity. Abalone is fished off the coasts in Sydney and was cheaper than what one would find elsewhere, but still more expensive than the other seafood in the market. At AUD10, we could buy a small serving of the dish instead of a complete meal if we picked a different dish. However, Vivek didn't want to miss out and bought a cocktail abalone. It was served in the shell, with a sprinkling of greens and a sprinkle of fresh cheese on top. It appeared to have been cooked in the shell and the cheese had been baked on top using a blowtorch. We also bought oysters and grilled local barramundi to try out.

The outside deck on the pier looked more interesting than the closed area so we went to eat out by the water. The pier at the Sydney fish market is one of the most beautiful places in the world. A meal here under the cobalt blue skies, as you look out onto the ocean, is pure bliss.

Vivek began eating. Even though the abalone was cooked, it was easy to detect the saltiness and the light buttery flavour of the univalve.

Abalone, after a long search

Abalone was somewhere between scallop and squid in its texture, with a crunchiness that sounded like a conch.

The barramundi, a popular fish in Australia, was grilled in a lemon-butter sauce that brought out the sweetish flavour in the fish. The flesh was soft and had very few bones making it easy to eat.

As Vivek savoured his food, we suddenly realized why so many people had chosen to eat in the enclosed space inside. A swarm of seagulls was busy trying to scavenge their lunch. The milder ones swiped leftover food from nearby tables, but the more bold ones were busy attacking the diners who were still eating. Suddenly, we heard a loud commotion from behind us.

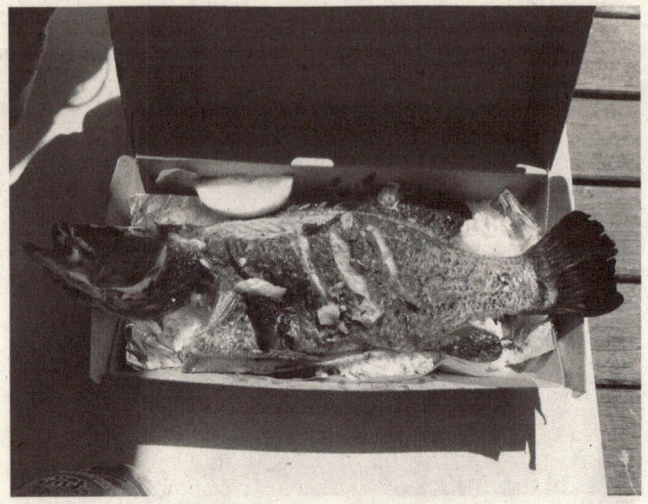

Fighting with the gulls over this barramundi

We turned just in time to see a crane jumping onto the table. It began feasting on the leftovers while the diners at the table had abandoned their food in shock. Since the humans had moved, the gulls closed in as well, but the crane was busy guarding its turf. Soon, there was a mini-war between the seagulls and the crane, which the crane was able to swiftly win and continue with its lunch.

I watched the entire spectacle awestruck. I wondered why Vivek wasn't philosophizing on whether the birds were eating our food or we were eating theirs, as he is often wont to do in such situations.

I turned around and saw that his survival instincts had kicked in, so he was busy shovelling in his food in a bid to ensure that he didn't lose out on his hard-earned lunch to bird wars.

Sydney Fish Market, Bank St and Pyrmont Beach Road			
Item	*Cocktail Abalone*	*Oysters*	*Grilled Barramundi*
Taste	★★★★★	★★★★	★★★
Price	AUD10	AUD2.5–3 each	AUD30
Fear Factor	3	3	1
New Species	Abalone	Oysters	Barramundi

Avenging Steve Irwin

After a few days in Sydney, we travelled to Cairns, Melbourne and Hobart in Tasmania. While we were in Cairns, we went to the Daintree Rainforest, the largest continuous tropical rainforest in Australia.[18] We saw many rare and poisonous trees and plants in the rainforest and also managed to spot a Southern Cassowary. The most important part of this trip, though, was getting to try out the classic Australian combination of Vegemite and damper.

A damper is a type of Australian soda bread. It was typically made by bushmen and travellers and involves baking the bread over the ashes of a campfire. The bread is dense and moist as compared to regular bread. It's also chewier and feels more glutinous in the mouth. A damper is eaten with butter and Vegemite, the famous Australian spread that is known to be an acquired taste. Vegemite is made from leftover brewers' yeast extract and is mixed with vegetables and spice additives. It tastes like its description, a hodgepodge of things thrown together into a spread and therefore a bit odd. We tried some of it straight out of the jar, which was strong and definitely an acquired taste, but it wasn't half bad when it was mixed with butter and spread onto the damper. I suspect the butter took the edge off. While it was an interesting experience, I doubt

I'll go back for more Vegemite. Or, maybe, I just need to eat it a few more times to love it as the Australians do!

~

After all our other travels, we were back in Sydney for a day before we flew back home. Vivek wanted to head back to Chinatown once last time because he had discovered a Malaysian restaurant that served stingray. Shreyas decided to join us so he could take me to his favourite laksa place which was also in the same area.

Once we got to the restaurant, Vivek immediately placed his order. Stingray takes a while to cook, about twenty minutes, so we passed the time chatting. When the stingray arrived, it was presented as a complete fin-shaped piece, contrary to our expectation that it would be served chopped into pieces. It was plated on a banana leaf, in typical Malay-style, with a slice of lemon, some peanut sauce and *sambal* on the side.

Vivek started examining the fish and pointing out how different stingray was from other fish.

'See how easily the meat is coming off, easily leaving this middle layer of cartilage. No other bones! It is like this creature evolved in order to be eaten at a restaurant,' he said as he ate it.

After a few more bites, he added, 'This cartilage is soft and edible, too. In a few minutes, I have made a whole stingray disappear without a trace!'

'So, how does it feel to strike one more off your list?' I asked him.

'Forget the list. This one is revenge for Steve Irwin,'* he replied.

---

* Steve Irwin, also known as 'The Crocodile Hunter', was an Australian zookeeper, conservationist and TV personality who died after being pierced by a stingray barb

Hawker Malaysian, 760 George Street, Haymarket	
Item	*Stingray*
Taste	★★★★★
Price	AUD16
Fear Factor	3
New Species	Stingray

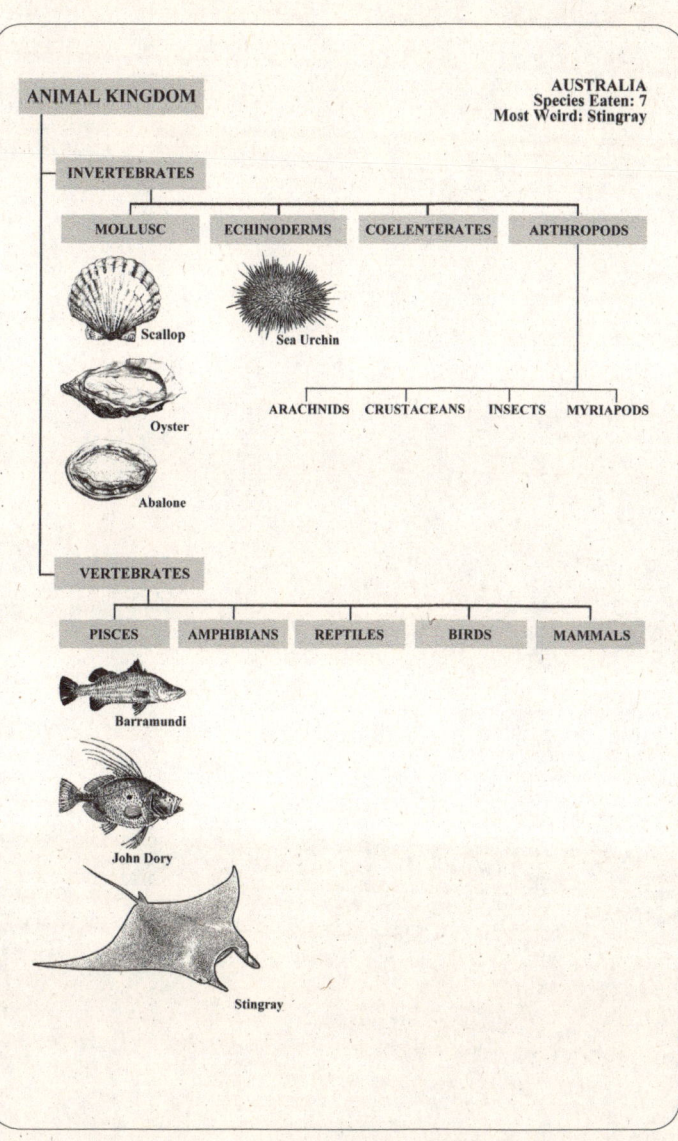

ANIMAL KINGDOM

AUSTRALIA
Species Eaten: 7
Most Weird: Stingray

INVERTEBRATES

MOLLUSC   ECHINODERMS   COELENTERATES   ARTHROPODS

Scallop

Sea Urchin

Oyster

ARACHNIDS   CRUSTACEANS   INSECTS   MYRIAPODS

Abalone

VERTEBRATES

PISCES   AMPHIBIANS   REPTILES   BIRDS   MAMMALS

Barramundi

John Dory

Stingray

CAMBODIA

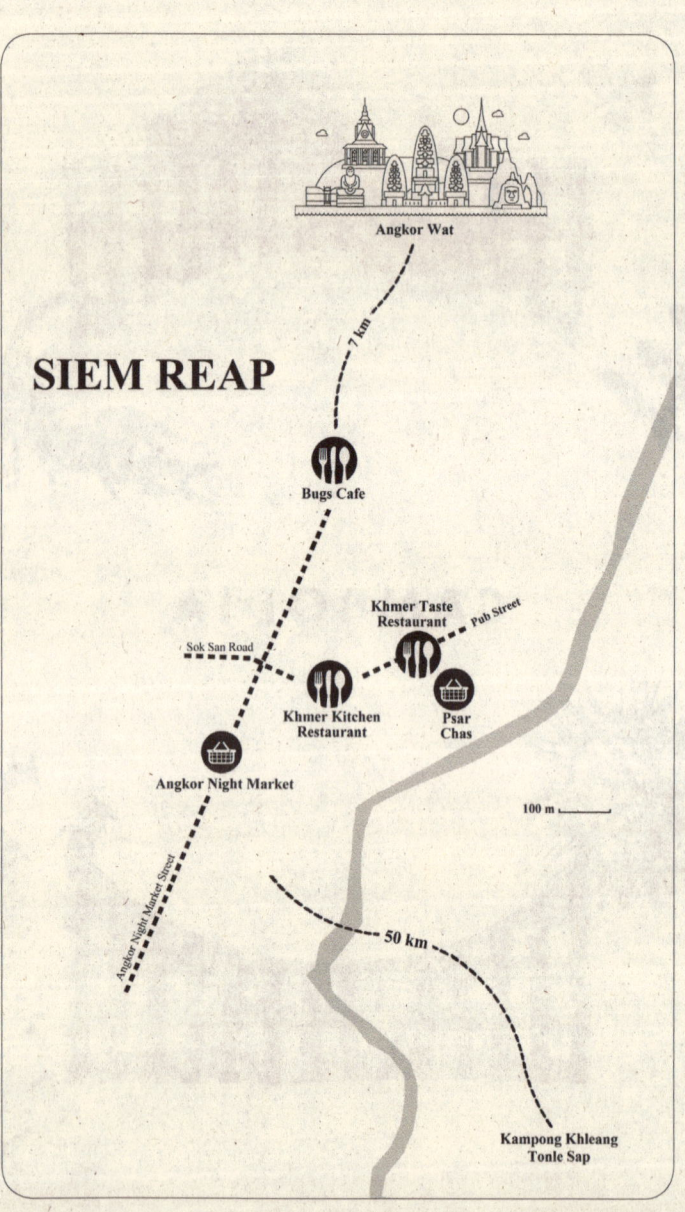

SIEM REAP

Angkor Wat

7 km

Bugs Cafe

Khmer Taste
Restaurant

Pub Street

Sok San Road

Khmer Kitchen
Restaurant

Psar
Chas

100 m

Angkor Night Market

Angkor Night Market Street

50 km

Kampong Khleang
Tonle Sap

As the sun rises behind the magnificent Angkor Wat, a collective gasp arises from the throngs of tourists waiting for this moment. This site is one of the biggest reasons why every traveller must visit Cambodia at least once in a lifetime. Angkor Wat is the largest religious monument in the world. It dates back to the twelfth century and was once at the centre of the Angkor Empire.[19] The temple complex is an architectural feat and home to many breathtaking structures. The complex is so large and overwhelming that there are tour passes available for one, three and even seven day visits.

I first visited Cambodia in the '90s as a pre-teen at a time when Siem Reap was the only tourist destination and Angkor Wat was nowhere near as crowded as it is today. Now, tourists have the option of visiting the capital city of Phnom Penh and the beautiful beaches at Koh Rong (Rabbit Island), Koh Thmei, Koh Ta Kiev and Koh Totang. One can also go on birding and wildlife tours, or visit the elephant sanctuaries at Mondulkiri in the Siem Reap province. We were in Cambodia to soak in the history and to try out the local Khmer cuisine. So, we decided to visit Siem Reap and Phnom Penh, both of which offered a good mix of history, as well as various markets that would aid food discoveries. Khmer, officially Angkor, was the predecessor to modern Cambodia and a powerful Hindu–Buddhist empire in Southeast Asia.

Khmer cuisine is all about contrasting tastes—sweet and bitter, salty and sour and fresh and cooked. It shares many commonalities with the neighbouring Thai and Vietnamese cuisines, however, it uses lesser sugar, chilli and coconut cream for flavour. Khmer food tends to contain a larger quantity of stir-fried vegetables and more garlic than Thai food. It also draws upon Chinese and French influences, both countries that have played key roles in Cambodian history. The curry dishes in Cambodia also have a strong Indian influence—probably why Khmer food was also our favourite since it appealed to our Indian palates!

Since Cambodia is home to the Mekong and Tonle Sap rivers, water, rice and freshwater fish are staples of Khmer cuisine, as seen in fish *amok*, the dish most synonymous with the country. The secret ingredient in all Khmer food is *prahok*—a salty, pungent paste made from fermented fish. Prahok is sometimes served in banana leaves and eaten on its own, but it is usually added to other dishes to add a kick and is an acquired taste. That basically makes even the most innocuous of Cambodian dishes quite adventurous in flavour!

The cheapest way to eat adventurously in Cambodia is at the local markets. We planned to spend time at all the large markets in Siem Reap and Phnom Penh through our five-day trip to ensure we sampled a broad variety of local dishes.

Fry, Little Bird, Fry!

Psar Chas, or the Old Market, is a labyrinthine market in the centre of Siem Reap. It is by the banks of the Stung Siem Reap river. Every morning, the locals head to Psar Chas to shop for everything from fresh produce to household items, to clothes and more. The food area is the greatest attraction at the Old Market—it is right in the middle and gives a glimpse into the real Cambodia.

Psar Chas was very close to our hotel, Diamond D'Angkor. I wondered out loud how Vivek always seemed to find us hotels that are super close to local markets. He claims it's serendipity but it seems like he plans this. Midway through our walk, I spotted a roadside restaurant advertising their 'Special amok curry'. I was hungry and I wasn't sure how long it would take before we reached the food section of the market. I was also eager to taste amok curry since it was the local specialty of Cambodia, so I jumped at the opportunity and suggested a pit stop.

'Amok' is the process of steam cooking a curry in banana leaves, which means that all amok curries are presented in a banana leaf bowl. Amok curry is the Cambodian equivalent of the south Indian elai saapadu, where food is served on a banana leaf plate. The classic Khmer amok curry is fish amok, made with prahok. Vivek didn't order as he wanted to first survey the varieties offered by the market. So, we got the vegetarian amok curry for me.

The curry was slightly sweet and had a custard-like consistency. I enjoyed the subtle play of flavours that the lemongrass and kaffir lime added to it. The key to a good amok curry is to find a restaurant that prepares it in the traditional manner and steams it within the banana leaf—most restaurants these days skip that step as it takes about twenty minutes. If the restaurant skips this step, you won't find the custard-like consistency that is so intrinsic to a good amok curry. All amok curries also include prahok, so let the restaurant know in advance if you're vegetarian.

Khmer Kitchen, Corner of 2 Thnou Street and Street 09	
Item	*Vegetarian Amok Curry*
Taste	★★★★★
Price	$4
Fear Factor	1
New Species	None

~

We resumed our walk towards Psar Chas, a covered open-air market tightly packed with vendors. The market is on the south side of the old French Quarter and very close to Pub Street. The location makes it a great place to shop and then head out for a walk by the river. We didn't know about the river when we got there as we entered from the opposite side of the market. It was a pleasant surprise when we exited from the other end and saw the river.

The periphery of the market was filled with hardware and houseware stores. At the entrance, we saw vendors selling traditional souvenirs and handicrafts like Khmer silk, perfumes, carvings, jewellery, silver and spices. Further inside the market were the vendors selling fruits, vegetables, meats and fresh seafood.

Our noses led us to the food section. The sickly sweet smell of the durian fruit filled the air. The produce section was on the periphery of the meat section. Since it was late in the day, many vendors had already sold their freshest stock. We walked on and were soon rewarded with the whiff of fresh meat almost immediately.

We were greeted by a large variety of sausages and other dried meats hanging from the entrance of the stalls. It was cramped, with very little space to move about. I was forewarned by my experiences at Khlong Toei Market in Bangkok and knew that I should look straight ahead to avoid accidentally making eye contact with a creature that was about to meet its maker. Meanwhile, Vivek went around scoping the stalls and was disappointed that all he could spot were chickens and ducks.

Suddenly, I spotted a food stall selling Cambodian dancing shrimps, a popular South Cambodian delicacy. Dancing shrimps are served alive in a clay pot and you need quick reflexes to be able to catch them and pop them into your mouth before they jump off your spoon and onto your lap! I was sure that Vivek would want to eat this. After all, what could be fresher than still alive seafood? To my surprise, he flatly refused! He clarified that he did not want to eat raw seafood because of all the toxins that marine creatures have consumed from the waste dumped into the oceans. We walked on to find something that wasn't tainted by human pollution.

Soon, we were well into the meat section and were confronted with various animal heads perched on shelves, stretching through the lengths of the aisles. It was almost as if a hunter had decided to display all his prized kills in one morbid corridor.

'See how happy those pigs look,' said Vivek, pointing at a shelf that was lined with pig heads.

My benchmark of pigs come from two sources—the cutesy illustrations of happy pink pigs in books and the ones you see eating trash by the side of the road. Neither of these could really explain where the pig heads in the market ranked as far as a real-world pig's emotions were concerned.

'Are you sure you're not projecting your own happiness on those pigs? How can they be happy if they're dead?' I asked.

'I have observed this very carefully, the pig heads always look happy in these counters,' said Vivek, with the all-knowing air of someone who has analysed many a pig head on many shelves in many meat markets across the world.

I wondered if this was a marketing trick employed by the pork industry, to trick people into buying and consuming their wares. Maybe people feel happier if they think the heads looked happy?

As we walked down the aisles, the raw stench of meat reduced and I started noticing baskets of insects placed along the sides of the alley. I wondered out loud if we were now in the insect section. But Vivek ignored me as he kept moving ahead with a sense of deep purpose. Suddenly, it struck me that he was possibly on a mission to find the paddy rats. I bit down on my questions as I wasn't sure if I wanted to be proved right. And that's when I almost stumbled into a stall that had what looked like big, wet blocks of dark chocolate displayed by the side.

'Look! That guy is selling chocolate,' I exclaimed in excitement.

'That's not chocolate, that's blood pudding, coagulated pig's blood,' Vivek clarified, much to my dismay.

I realized I was reaching the limits of my ability to stay. Like travellers in the desert conjure up the mirage of an oasis, I was beginning to see visions of dark chocolate in a meat market. The disappointment at discovering my dark chocolate haven was coagulated blood sickened me a little, so I suggested that we take a break and go sit by the river. However, Vivek did not think it was very prudent to cut short his explorations.

So, I left to go sit by the river and he went back to the meat section to complete his search. I found a wide bench where I could get some fresh air and go back to the book I was carrying with me. Within a few minutes, Vivek emerged from the market with a triumphant grin, holding aloft a half-open takeaway container that looked like it had onion pakodas in it.

'Are those pakodas,' I asked hopefully, even though I knew that despite the plethora of Indian restaurants we'd spotted in Siem Reap, there was zero chance that the meat section of Psar Chas would have yielded this. I was hoping that maybe he had taken a quick detour to get me something because the dreams of dark chocolate had made me hungry.

'Look closer,' he said, and that's when I realized that each of those supposed pakodas had a head, a small bird body and a beak. They were fried sparrows, a delicacy in Cambodia. Many of Cambodia's indigenous plants were wiped out during the Khmer Rouge reign of terror. In a country where there weren't many choices for food, birds like sparrows, which are easy to catch and where every part can be consumed, quickly became a part of the culinary repertoire.

'I call this serendipity,' Vivek said as he unpacked his fried sparrow. 'I was not expecting to find sparrows here. I was only looking for the rats.'

The sparrows were served with a side of pepper and lemon wedges. He began eating them with medical precision, pulling apart the meat bit by bit so he could figure out what each individual part tasted like. Vivek was able to ensure that he salvaged every bit of the tasty meat from the tiny bird. Unlike fried chicken, where only the exterior is fried, here the meat was fried to the bone.

I went back to my book, wishing I had some pakodas to eat.

Psar Chas Market, Psar Chas Road	
Item	*Fried Sparrow*
Taste	★★★★
Price	$5
Fear Factor	4
New Species	Sparrow

~

Later that evening, we explored the night market. Due to the influx of tourists in Siem Reap over the years, there are many night markets. The original night market is Angkor Night Market on Sivatha Road. We soon realized that it was mostly filled with stalls catering to tourists, with souvenirs and other tchotchkes, the most interesting of which were bottles of snake wine and scorpion wine. We didn't spot many food stalls so we went to Pub Street, the Siem Reap equivalent of Bangkok's Khao San Road.

Pub Street was lively and beautiful, with fairy lights twinkling along the road. Large signs advertised food, pubs and live performances. Most tourists were making a bee-line towards 'Angkor What?' and 'Temple', the two most popular bars. We were more interested in the carts lined up along the side of the road, with their giant displays of insects of all shapes and sizes.

Alcohol with extra bite

Vivek had learned from past experiences and examined the wares at every cart before he narrowed down on one that had the best 'quality' of insects. The highlight of this cart was the tarantulas.

As he began evaluating the tarantulas, we were joined by a Belgian couple who appeared to be on a similar quest. Vivek and the Belgian man immediately struck up a friendship and began discussing the merits of the tarantulas in the cart, in the manner of seasoned tarantula purchasers. Meanwhile, I began chatting with the woman who told me they'd been in Cambodia for a week and they had visited Phnom Penh and then travelled down to Siem Reap via Battambang on a boating trip. They also mentioned that they'd managed to get one of the locals on the boat to help them source rats. Vivek couldn't control his excitement. He suggested we look for a boat tour of our own and change our plans, but I had to remind him that we were on a short trip and the chances of a ten-hour plus boat ride were next to none. He let go of that idea and went back to finding the right tarantula. Both men selected a tarantula each.

Pub Street: Bugs of your choice

The tarantula legs were dry, wooden stick-like in texture, like long *sev bhujia*. The stomach and body were juicier and had skin similar to that of grapes according to the local insect expert, Vivek. It amazes me that he can think of tarantulas, bhujia and grapes in a single thought.

As I pondered over that, he added, 'Tarantulas are venomous. You know that, right?'

I stared at him while he licked the last of the flavour from his fingers, looking none the worse for the wear.

I later realized he was showing off. Tarantula has been eaten in Cambodia for centuries. The locals say that while tarantulas are venomous, their venom is intended for smaller prey and transmitted through bites and hence there's no problem with eating them.

Vivek was glad that the insects here weren't overly fried such that the taste was lost. The Belgian couple moved on and Vivek asked the cart owner where he could find some paddy rats. She said that like many other foods that are commonly eaten in the Cambodian villages, rats were also very hard to find in the cities though they were still consumed in the villages. She was clear that she couldn't help with this quest. We would have to look elsewhere. We decided to go back to the hotel because we were planning an early start the next morning to watch the sunrise at Angkor Wat.

Insect Cart, Pub Street	
Item	*Fried Tarantulas*
Taste	★★★★
Price	$1–2, depending on size
Fear Factor	5
New Species	Tarantula

~

On the way back, we stopped at Khmer Taste restaurant to have dinner. I hadn't eaten anything yet and while the tarantulas were good enough to feed the mind, Vivek also needed more physical sustenance. While I quickly settled on some fried rice, Vivek spent some time perusing the menu and discovered that they were serving roasted frogs.

During the Khmer Rouge regime, people were forced to survive on a diet of *borbor* or rice porridge.[20] During the monsoons, frogs were abundant and even though it was illegal to eat anything but borbor at the time, people began consuming them as a rich source of protein. Thus, frogs became an integral part of the local diet and cuisine. Today, deep fried and grilled bullfrogs are legally available all over Cambodia and are a must-have on the list of any adventurous eater.

The roasted frogs were definitely the star dish. The frogs were juicy and tasted a lot like a slimy version of white meat, like chicken. They are less fibrous and have a deeper taste. The sliminess is just a reference to the texture and not in any way a reflection on the taste!

'Do you realize that all the meat in a frog is on the thighs? No wonder they can jump up to twenty times their size,' Vivek said as he picked up one of the frogs and laid it out on the plate like the Vitruvian man.

If the first day in Cambodia was an indicator of things to come, with the tarantulas and frogs, then this trip was going to have many serendipitous discoveries of adventurous foods.

Khmer Taste, Sok San Road, Near Pub Street	
Item	*Roasted Frogs*
Taste	★★★★★
Price	$5
Fear Factor	4
New Species	Frog

Excuse Me! There's Food in My Bugs!

We spent most of our second morning in Siem Reap at the temples of Angkor Wat. We left before dawn so we could find a good spot to watch the sunrise. As the sun rises, the mirror image of the temple is visible in stages in the pond that's directly in front of it. When the sun is up, there's a perfectly symmetrical view of the temple intersecting with its reflection. It's nearly impossible to describe the awe-inspiring beauty of the temple.

Once the sun was up, we explored the interiors of the main temple complex. Angkor Wat is astounding with entire galleries that depict elaborately etched scenes from epics like the Ramayana and Mahabharata. My personal favourite was the spectacular wall that depicts a multitude of scenes from the war in Lanka. It's mind-boggling to think of the creative effort it would've taken to produce such painstakingly detailed renditions of scenes. It took us a few hours to go around the entire complex of the main temple, after which we moved to the other temples.

We visited Angkor Thom, about a kilometre away from the north entrance to Angkor Wat. The five entry towers of this temple are the most photographed of all the ruins. Each sandstone tower is about twenty-three metres high and is crowned with one head facing a cardinal direction. Within the complex, right at the centre, is the temple of Bayon. Over 200 large faces carved into the fifty-four towers give this temple its character. The reliefs on the outer gallery of Bayon are generic scenes of everyday life, with pictures of markets, fishing, festivals, battles and processions. North of Bayon is Baphuon with more than ten chambers at its base. We walked down the gallery near the East tower so we could get a view of the Bayon framed by the doorway of the Baphuon.

From here, we went to the temple of Ta Phrom, popularly known as the 'Tomb Raider' temple, because it featured in the movie.[21] The trees growing through the walls in many parts of this temple give an aura of strength and long-lasting grandeur to it. Our last stop was the red sandstone temple at Banteay Srei. It's thirty minutes away by tuk-tuk and I was particularly interested in it because the architectural style is closer to Indian temples than the others in the region. The temple is situated in the heart of a forest. By the time we were done exploring Banteay Srei, we were exhausted, especially because it had been getting much hotter. The heat is one reason why many tourists opt for three or seven-day passes so they can see the temples at leisure during the early hours of the morning. Our express run through of the main temples was tiring.

Later that evening, we went back to the centre of all activity in Siem Reap: Pub Street. We enjoyed walking around the well-lit streets and watching live music performances happening at the open-air restaurants in the area. Pub Street comes alive late in the evening when the night markets begin. That night, we first planned to visit a tapas bar that was on top of Vivek's list of places to eat at in Cambodia.

Bugs Café is a tapas bar with a twist. It is the brainchild of David Blouzard, a Frenchman who wants people to experience eating bugs in a non-intimidating manner. The Cambodians began eating insects during the time of the Khmer Rouge. Spiders, crickets, grasshoppers and water beetles were an important source of energy to the millions of malnourished locals during Pol Pot's regime. Insects are a village food and it's hard to find restaurants that sell a local version, outside of the carts at the night markets. The carts are intimidating because of how they display the varying types of insects in their full glory. Bugs Café seeks to break down the mental barrier of eating insects, by incorporating them into food that's familiar.

The interiors of the cafe have a European vibe and there's both indoor and outdoor seating. David meets every customer himself and takes you through the philosophy of the restaurant before recommending dishes. He told us that he hired a French chef to ensure that every dish incorporated the right insect flavours and nothing tastes odd or out of place.

I've already decided to survive any apocalypse by eating seaweed, the vegetarian equivalent of insects.[22] It's available in abundance, doesn't require much energy to produce and is a rich source of protein for plant-eaters. When the end of the world arrives, you'll find me snacking on seaweed strips while Vivek starts selling cricket bhujia made from the cricket farm he plans to set up. So, I let Vivek experience the Bugs Café insect menu, while I opted for the non-insect versions.

David generally recommends the tapas platter as a good way to taste the various insects they offer in one go. Vivek had already had many insects in the platter like water bugs, crickets and tarantulas. After a lot of deliberation, he opted for Bee Larvae Soup and Flying Ants Salad.

The Flying Ants Salad arrived first. It looked like a Mediterranean salad at any good restaurant. It had fresh cucumbers, tomatoes, olives and a dash of feta cheese. When you looked closely, you noticed that it also included a liberal sprinkling of flying ants. The restaurant does a brilliant job at integrating the insects. As I looked at that salad, I realized what David meant when he said that his food is a gateway to insect consumption. Unlike the insect carts that sold insects by the kilo, this was an unassuming dish that incorporated them well.

Flying Ants Salad at Bugs Café: The tastiest bugs can look

The second course was the Bee Larvae Pumpkin Soup and much to Vivek's delight, it also included some bees that were still attached to a part of the honeycomb. There were brownish-black chunks floating in the yellow soup. A passing glance would make you think that there was an odd vegetable floating around, however, a closer look would tell you that this was bee larva in your soup!

Vivek wanted to see the comb in its full glory, so he requested David to bring some uncooked combs out from the kitchen. As we looked closely at the comb, we saw that these bees were still attached to a cross section of the honeycomb and that's what led to the chunky appearance in the soup.

Bee Larvae Soup: Don't miss the croutons

Bees 101: A cross-section of the hive

Both the salad and the soup were extremely tasty, a testament to the skills of the chef. The salad was light, with an added crispiness from the flying ants. Most of us would have ingested ants at some point in time, at least the small ones that roam around everywhere. Some of us may have also eaten ants when trying to snack on sugar from the tin before our parents spotted us. They have a tangy taste, somewhat like unripe berries. The ants on the salad tasted the same. They were partly crunchy and partly squishy and this went well with the vegetables in the salad. Vivek even went so far as to remark that he could get used to eating ants and it's time the grocery stores started stocking them.

The soup was thick and creamy. It was extremely flavourful. Vivek said that the bees added additional flavour to the soup. The larvae had a soft yet solid exterior and a creamy interior. Vivek was unable to compare it to anything else—after all, there aren't too many things similar to a honeycomb with baby bees nestled within. He enjoyed both dishes and would've likely ordered a few more if he wasn't so full.

When I asked him if these were the best insect dishes he'd tried, he said, 'Other than the ant bhurji, this was easily the best. The only thing that would top this would be going into a Cambodian village and eating insects caught in the wild and cooked Khmer-style at someone's home!'

We haven't yet managed a trip into the villages, but if you ever spot a 'Keeda Café' in Bangalore, I recommend you check to see if the proprietor is named Vivek Singh. I'm still debating which of these dishes would taste better—Cheenti Chicken Tikka or a bee-chutney to go with Crunchy Cricket Dosas?

Vivek, however, has a very clear opinion—'Excuse me! There's food in my bugs! Can I have my bugs on the side?'

Bugs Café, 351 Thmey Village, Angkor Night Market Road		
Item	*Flying Ants Salad*	*Bee Larvae Soup*
Taste	★★★★★	★★★★★
Price	$6	$5
Fear Factor	5	5
New Species	Flying Ants	Bee Larvae

~

We went back to Pub Street to inspect the insect carts again. We stopped at one and saw many of the wares we'd seen before—tarantulas, worms of all kinds, snakes and frogs. The snake was twisted in an S-shape, with a long bamboo skewer through the centre. Even though he had eaten water snake in Bangkok, Vivek decided to get this one.

The meat was centred towards the length of the spine. It looked more aesthetic than the ones in Bangkok, which had been fried out of shape. This snake was mounted fully on the skewer, so it looked like the fried snake was looking at you while you ate it. The skin glistened, not from oil, but from the texture of the skin. The skin was tough, as is the case with most reptiles. It was salty in taste. The flesh under the skin had also shrunk while it was fried and got stuck to the bones. The final result was the taste of chicken skin stuck on thin, fine bone, that needed to be scraped off. He ended up wishing there was either more flesh or a way to scrape all of it off the bones. Despite being someone who otherwise manages to extract meat out of every crevice of every creature, he regretfully ended up throwing some of it away.

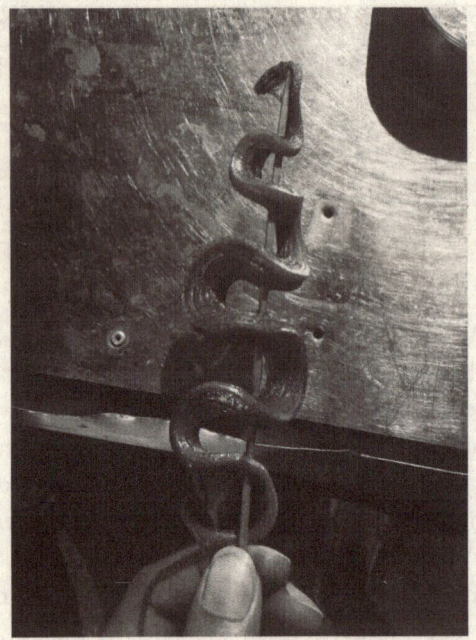

Snake on a stick

Insect Cart, Pub Street	
Item	*Snake*
Taste	★★★
Price	$2
Fear Factor	5
New Species	Snake

~

Vivek continued to chat with vendors in Pub Street to see if he could locate a rat. Finally, he found a vendor towards the end of the street who told him that he could bring rats the next day.

'Come back at 7.30 p.m. tomorrow and I will have a rat,' he said.

Vivek clarified that this would be a cooked rat. Then, he delved deeper into the source of the rat.

'I heard that most Cambodians only eat rats in the village. Is there a village nearby from where you're getting me this rat?'

'Yes, I will catch it and bring it,' said the vendor.

Vivek asked him a few more questions about how he would catch the rat, which nearby village he'd catch the rat from and so on. The vendor kept repeating that we needed to come back there the next day. Vivek was seeking out some specific information that he wasn't getting. Finally, he looked semi-convinced and I thought he would close the deal. To my surprise, he said, 'Okay, thank you, but I don't think we will be back tomorrow. I have a flight to catch at 8.00 p.m.'

As we walked away, I asked him, 'Why did you say that? Our flight is much later, we could've made it here at 7.30 p.m.'

'No, I don't want to eat the rat he will bring.'

'But, why? He said he'll cook it and you've been talking about the rat you missed in Bangkok for over a year,' I said.

'Cambodian villagers eat rats they catch in their fields,' he said. 'The rats in the villages grow up eating paddy from the fields. What if this guy was planning to catch a rat from his home. That will be a city rat that grew up eating sewage. The only way I will eat a rat is if the rat and all its previous generations have lived in fields and grew up on the good stuff. I can't even imagine eating a sewer rat. I might be weird but I'm not disgusting!'

Keep Clam and Carry On

Tonlé Sap, one of the largest freshwater lakes in Asia,[23] is a popular destination in Cambodia, second only to Angkor Wat. The huge dumbbell shaped water body stretches across the northwest side of the country. Visiting the Tonlé Sap is like visiting a different Cambodia, one that involves floating villages, cultural and nature tours and bird watching. Of the many floating villages, Chong Kneas is the most popular. We considered going to both Kompong Khleang, a village on stilts, or Kampong Phluk, a floating village. The locals recommend both of these for those interested in an authentic experience. They both sounded interesting, but we picked Kompong Khleang for being the least visited and because we wanted to see the houses on stilts.

The journey started with a drive from Siem Reap to the docks, which took us through a large part of the countryside. We were surrounded by large green fields and tiny houses dotted along the periphery in the distance. At the docks, we got on a motorized longboat with wooden seats. The water levels were low because we were travelling in the middle of summer when the river shrinks to one-fourth its size. The boat got stuck in the mud a few times as we made our way down the river. We weren't quite clear how we'd get out of the sludge and to the river. Thankfully, we were helped by locals on fishing boats.

We floated down the river that was surrounded by houses perched on stilts on either side. During the monsoons, when the water level is higher, the houses look like they're floating on the river. Every house had pigs in pens and chicken coops suspended off the stilts. There were women washing clothes off the edge of their porch and children playing around them.

We soon pulled up at the village dock. There was a central lane through the market area of the village. As we entered the lane, we saw a street cart selling something that looked like groundnuts. There were piled in large mounds and a group of school children was busy buying plastic packets filled with them. We went closer and discovered that these were actually bite-sized clams. Since Kompong Khleang is a fishing village, these were freshwater clams from the river nearby.

'No, not peanuts. Give me a bag of clams!'

Vivek joined the children in haggling with the vendor and got everyone a bulk discount. The children were very amused to see someone who wasn't a local eat the clams and gave Vivek directions on how to open the clams and eat them. It looked like hard work since each tiny clam had to be prised open and the meat sucked out of it. They were flavoured with chilli oil. Vivek could taste the freshness and he enjoyed the blend of the salty clams with the chilli oil used in the seasoning. Vivek tried offering it to the other travellers in our group, but none of them were brave enough to try them out.

Roadside Cart, Kampong Khleang Floating Village	
Item	*Steamed Clams*
Taste	★★★
Price	$0.25
Fear Factor	3
New Species	Clams

~

As we continued our walk, we saw large sheets on which prawns and shrimps were being dried in the sun. They were laid out on bamboo sheets, with smoke nearby. It reminded me of how papads are dried on the rooftops during the Indian summer. Much of the seafood found in Siem Reap comes from the adjoining fishing villages. Our guide told us that the dried prawns and shrimps are preserved, flavoured and then boxed for sale.

From the village, we took another boat to go further into the Tonlé Sap River to a floating restaurant. It was a beautiful ride with thick lush jungles on either side. The floating restaurant was at the point where the river got so wide that it seemed like we were out at sea. It was on a boat that had a crocodile cage on the side. The crocodile viewing is a much-advertised portion of a trip to Kampong Khleang, though it was very zoo-like to me. The crocodile is enclosed within a cage underwater and visitors can go out on to the deck of the boat to view it. We had read that there are crocodile farms in the region which process crocodile meat. But we didn't see it on any menu here. Vivek didn't ask about it because he didn't want to inadvertently ask the owner if we could eat his pet crocodile.

Especially not when we were on an artificial two-room island in the middle of nowhere.

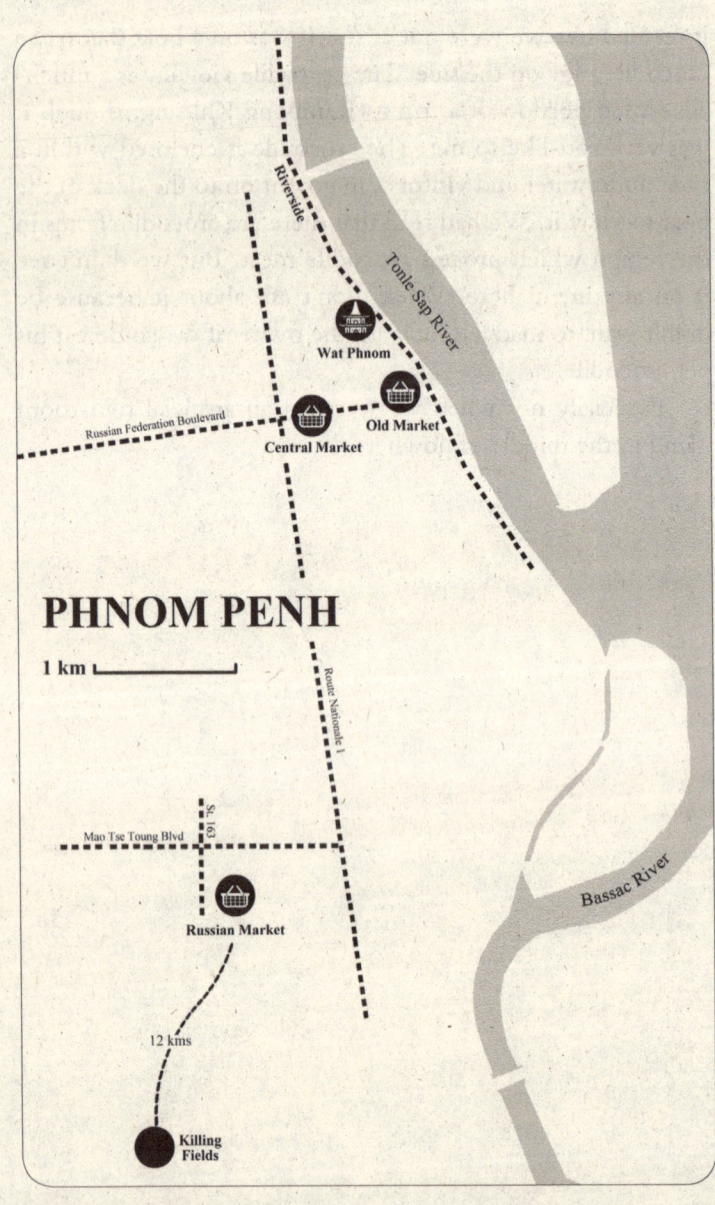

PHNOM PENH

1 km

Riverside

Tonle Sap River

Wat Phnom

Central Market

Old Market

Russian Federation Boulevard

Route Nationale 1

St. 163

Mao Tse Toung Blvd

Russian Market

12 kms

Killing Fields

Bassac River

Nom Nom Phnom Penh

Phnom Penh conjures up images of glittering gold spires, large rivers, a populous capital city, French colonial mansions and tree-lined boulevards amongst Angkor-style architecture. It is located on the banks of the Tonlé Sap and Mekong rivers. It is well-noted for its architectural beauty.[24] The city gets its name from Wat Phnom, which means 'Hill Temple'. It is a city filled with markets, so it's hard to pick one to visit. We decided to explore the Old Market because it houses the best food market in the area and follow that up with a visit to the Russian Market, which our hotel receptionist recommended as a good place to find souvenirs.

The Old Market is housed in a beautiful art-deco building. It is dome-shaped, with four arms branching out into hallways stocked with innumerable goods. There are different sections for every item—aisles of apparel, housewares, souvenirs, personal care items and more. The central area houses jewellery, often touted as one of the key reasons to visit. Unlike other tourists, we were most interested in exploring the fresh food section and so with just a cursory glance in the direction of the jewellery section, we headed towards the food.

The air near the food section had a fishy odour that I later discovered was the smell of shrimp in brine. Various animal body parts and live fish were being sold along the aisles. Many of the stalls in the open-air area were shut because it had been raining heavily all morning.

We also walked through the souvenir section of the market but didn't purchase anything. Interestingly, many of the stalls had signs urging tourists not to buy 'temple stones' as a souvenir. The signs called out that these are often fake and also drew attention to the fact that buying a genuine piece of temple stone would damage the local architecture.

We walked around for a few hours, but we didn't spot any new species so we decided to stop at the Russian Market on the way back. While we didn't eat at the Old Market, it is still highly recommended for shopping and for the food stalls within the market all of which have a wide variety of local dishes to try out.

~

The Russian Market is in the south of Phnom Penh. From the outside, it did not have the same presence as the Old Market. In fact, the building was quite nondescript. It is, however, a bustling market within and has everything from DVDs, fake apparel and bags, to hand-carved statues, lanterns and handmade silk scarves. We were hungry so we went straight to the food stalls.

The food stalls were clustered in the centre of the market. The market was already warm and the steam from the cooking made this area even warmer. We walked around looking at the menus of all the stalls. At one of the stalls, we found a fried shrimp baguette, Cambodian style.

The fried shrimp baguette really brings out the French influences on Cambodian cooking. The baguette is topped with shrimp and deep-fried. The shrimp is cooked Khmer style, with three different sauces. Vivek took a bite and was surprised to realize that there were still crunchy pieces of shell on the shrimp. Since the shrimp were small, the shells were edible. Over time, he got used to the texture and eventually pronounced it to be truly delicious and a must try dish if you're in Phnom Penh.

Shrimp baguette: Can we make this at home?

Food Stall, Russian Market, Corner of Street 163 and Street 444	
Item	*Fried Bread and Shrimp*
Taste	★★★
Price	$0.25
Fear Factor	2
New Species	None

~

We also spotted crab, prawns and even grilled squid, lightly marinated in lime juice or fish sauce. Grilled squid is a highly recommended Cambodian street food, but Vivek decided to skip this. We stopped at Sarang Foods for lunch. There were a lot of people eating there, a clear indicator that the food was going to be good. The stall had a central assembly area with tables and chairs placed all around it. We both decided to have some *kuy teav*, Cambodian noodle soup. The broth used in Cambodian soup is darker and thicker than what is found in the neighbouring country of Vietnam. The soup was garnished with bean sprouts and herbs. We had a choice of condiments on the side—chilli sauce, soy sauce, pepper, lime and garlic. The stall owner didn't understand English, so we pointed at the dishes and sides we wanted to get our soups. The soups were very tasty and filling. We both like lemongrass, a key ingredient in most local foods in Cambodia and the soup was no exception to its abundance.

~

That evening, we went to the Phnom Penh riverside. This river, in downtown Phnom Penh, is actually a part of the Tonlé Sap River. The avenue that goes through the river is called Preah Sisowath, in honour to King Sisowath. We walked on the pier area by the river and then crossed over to sit at one of the riverside cafes. The walkway near the river is 1 km in length and we walked along it for 5–6 hours taking breaks at the various restaurants, cafés and food stalls lined up along the other side of the road.

Once the sun began to set, we went back to the pier to where vendors had now begun setting up their stalls for the night-time food market. We surveyed all the food options. Vivek soon spotted one thing we hadn't seen thus far—fried balut.

Fried balut

The Cambodian version was batter fried and served with a dash of pepper. This local variety was definitely more palatable than the self-cooked version that Vivek attempted in Seattle. Fried balut looked like the egg pakodas that are sold on roadside pushcarts in smaller towns in India. The egg pakodas are made of boiled eggs that are batter fried. This balut was exactly like that, except that it tasted completely like balut.

Through our trip to Cambodia, we came across many of the foods that Cambodia is famous for—amok, tarantulas and other insects, snakes, balut and grilled frogs. However, a key characteristic of many Southeast Asian cultures is also the ability to cook every part of an animal, including the offal and innards. Vivek was yet to try either.

'Maybe I should start a branch of the chart for animal body parts,' he mused.

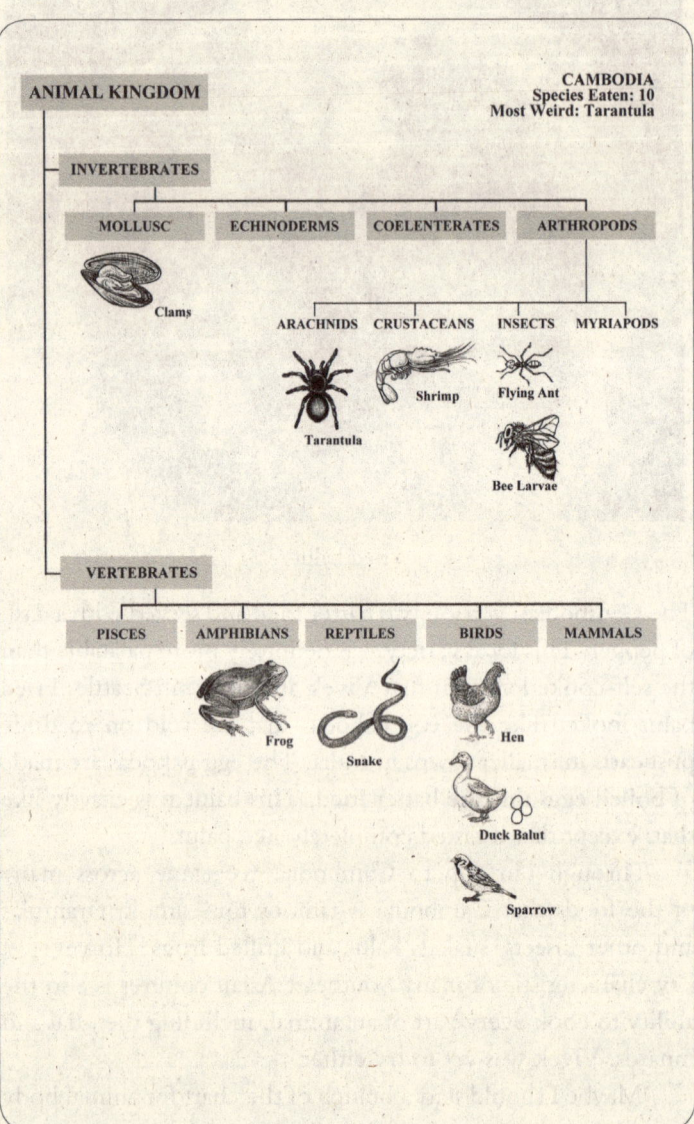

ANIMAL KINGDOM

CAMBODIA
Species Eaten: 10
Most Weird: Tarantula

INVERTEBRATES

MOLLUSC   ECHINODERMS   COELENTERATES   ARTHROPODS

Clams

ARACHNIDS   CRUSTACEANS   INSECTS   MYRIAPODS

Tarantula

Shrimp

Flying Ant

Bee Larvae

VERTEBRATES

PISCES   AMPHIBIANS   REPTILES   BIRDS   MAMMALS

Frog

Snake

Hen

Duck Balut

Sparrow

VIETNAM

Rice Paper Village

Cu Chi Tunnels

Cricket Farm

60 km

HO CHI MINH CITY

Notre Dame

Saigon
Central
Post Office

War Remnants
Museum

Independence
Palace

Nguyen Du

Nguyen Thi Minh Khai

Truong Dinh

Ben Thanh
Street Food Market

Barbecue
Garden

60 km

Le Thanh Ton

Ben Thanh Market

200 m

Mekong River
Delta

The dramatic landscapes, fascinating history and delicious food of Vietnam will draw you back again and again. From the picturesque World Heritage sites of Halong Bay, Phong Na Ke Bang caves, Hoi An ancient street and Cham Island, to the bustling cities of Hanoi and Ho Chi Minh, to the rice fields of Sapa and the beaches of Nha Trang and Phu Quoc, it's nearly impossible to decide which parts of Vietnam to skip. Even a few weeks seem like too little time to spend there. Street food is a key component of any trip to Vietnam and one can find many weird foods on the list of must-try dishes in Vietnam.

Vietnamese cuisine is an effortless balance of fragrance, taste and colour. Most Vietnamese dishes combine the five fundamental tastes—spicy, sour, bitter, salty and sweet, corresponding to the five elements metal, wood, fire, water and earth. While Vietnamese cuisine varies by region, the common characteristics include fresh vegetables and meats, herbs, variation in textures, broths and the use of colourful condiments to present the dish.

In northern Vietnam, the cold climate restricts the availability of spices, so the food is comparatively less spicy. Most dishes are subtle in their balance of flavours. There's greater use of seafood and most of the notable dishes are crab-based. Fish sauce, soy sauce and prawn sauce are the main flavouring ingredients. Signature dishes of Northern Vietnam are *bun rieu*,[*] *bun cha*[†] and *pho ga*.[‡]

---

[*] Meat rice vermicelli soup
[†] Rice with marinated pork
[‡] Rice noodle with chicken

The abundance of spices in Central Vietnam results in the spicy food found here. Hue, once the capital of the last dynasty, has highly decorative and colourful food, which reflects the influence of ancient Vietnamese royal cuisine. The most frequently used ingredients here are chilli peppers and shrimp sauce.

Southern Vietnam is warm and fertile, resulting in the growth of a wide variety of fruits and vegetables. The food is vibrant and colourful, with liberal use of garlic, shallots and fresh herbs. There's a preference for sweetness as seen in the liberal use of sugar in the sauces, as well as coconut milk in the curries.

Exploring Vietnam needs a longer trip, so we planned to be there for ten days, in December 2017. What we didn't realize was that even with that much time, we would barely be able to scratch the surface. We were able to cover both Northern and Southern Vietnam, but we weren't able to head to Central Vietnam. We spent our time looking for new dishes and stopping at the innumerable street-side stalls, so we did manage to try a wide variety of the local cuisine. However, Vietnam has not seen the last of us yet!

Spoilt for Choice

When you step off the plane into Ho Chi Minh City, you're hit by a wave of humidity followed by the usual sounds and lights of a bustling city. The most populated city in Vietnam, it's chaotic and dynamic with a complex history and plenty of culture to soak in. While the mopeds land up on the sidewalk in a manner similar to many crowded Indian cities, they far outnumber the cars. Therefore, the traffic looks less chaotic than what we are used to, especially coming from a city as crowded as Bangalore.

We got to our hotel before noon and couldn't check in right away. So, we left our luggage at the hotel reception and went looking for restaurants nearby. We walked a few blocks before we found Barbecue Garden, a restaurant that served hotpot. Hotpot is a Chinese soup typically prepared at the table. The broth is placed on a barbecue stove built into the table and the vegetables, noodles and meats are served on the side. You drop them into the broth and pick them out when they're cooked, so everyone gets a custom soup. Despite the heat, we decided to order it. Vivek was especially thrilled to discover that they had a seafood hotpot, which he ordered.

It had clams, jumbo prawns and scallops. The broth was flavourful and rather light. We spent a couple of hours savouring it. While you can find hotpot at some restaurants in India, this was Vivek's first time trying out a hotpot where he was cooking the meat himself. After we were done, we went back to check into our hotel and move on to seeing some of the local sights.

Hot pot with jumbo prawns

Barbecue Garden Restaurant, 35 Nam Kỳ Khởi Nghĩa, Phường Bến Thành	
Item	*Seafood Hot Pot*
Taste	★★★★
Price	₫288,000
Fear Factor	2
New Species	None

~

Later that afternoon, we went to the Notre Dame Cathedral, only to discover that it was shut, owing to renovations. The Cathedral is located in downtown Ho Chi Minh City and is a remnant of the French colonial history. From the outside, it strongly resembles its Parisian counterpart, with two bell towers each reaching a height of fifty-eight metres.[25] While we couldn't go in, the exteriors alone were majestic. We walked around the church for a while and then headed to the Central Post Office, which is right across the road. The post office is another remnant of the colonial era and is possibly the grandest post office in all of Southeast Asia.[26] The stately yellow building houses a large central hall with marble flooring, looping arches and antiquated telephone boxes. While the architectural style is distinctly French, the large portrait of Ho Chi Minh hanging high above the far end of the hall will instantly remind you of where you actually are. The building has strong historical significance but is also a functioning post office, so you will spot many tourists sending out postcards in a bid to experience living history. We walked around admiring the architecture, especially the ceiling, which has two maps of the region, one of which shows the telephone line crisscrossing between Vietnam and Cambodia and the other displaying a map of Saigon in the year 1892. From here, we headed to the War Remnants Museum.

The museum houses many exhibits from the First Indochina war involving the French colonialists, as well as from the more recent Vietnam War. It consists of themed rooms on several floors, with a central yard that displays military equipment. Exhibits include the 'tiger cages' in which the South Vietnamese government housed war criminals, as well as graphic photography highlighting the effects of Agent Orange, the use of napalm and phosphorous bombs and other war atrocities like the Mai Lai massacre. It is a chilling reminder of the aftermath of war on a country and its people. A visit to the museum is a sobering experience. We spent a few hours viewing the exhibits and then left to explore the markets.

Outside the museum, many of the souvenir shops were selling local snake and scorpion wines. The belief is that alcohol neutralizes the venom from the bites. Some Southeast Asian countries also believe the wine to have medicinal properties. We came across this in Cambodia as well. Surprisingly, I've never seen Vivek express interest despite the fact that he eats scorpions and snakes and also drinks wine!

~

We headed to Ben Thanh, the city's largest market. During the day, the market is alive with vendors selling their wares and fresh produce. We got there at around 6.30 p.m., which was a rather bad time as it meant that the market was shutting and the night market, that sets up outside the market building, wouldn't open for another half hour. We decided to visit Ben Thanh Street Food Market that was across the road to get some food while we waited for the night market to open.

Ben Thanh Street Food Market is a large building riddled with food stalls that are laid out in columns. As you pass by, the vendors call out to you to buy their dishes. There are open seating areas at the front and back of the enclosure. The seating area at the front is next to a large stage where there are musical performances over the weekend. This is a great place to experience local and other cuisines as you enjoy a live performance.

The first item that caught my attention here was Vietnamese pizza made on an open grill. The pizza base was thin, almost papad-like. As it began to cook, a quail egg was broken on it, followed by adding sauces, veggies and meats, as per customer preference. The last step was cooking it with a blowtorch to bake it all in from the top.

Vietnamese pizza

The same stall also had pork and chicken cooked within a hollowed out bamboo stem, a local delicacy that was attracting a lot of customers. I considered buying something right away, but we decided to explore the market in full before we made our decision.

A little ahead, I spotted a stall with a wide variety of seafood listed on the many menus tacked to the wall. To supplement the menus, there were posters of things I hadn't seen before so I knew this stall offered a variety of new dishes. It also had large aquariums with many creatures floating around in them which I pointed out to Vivek. His eyes lit up as he skimmed through the menu. The stall had a wide variety of snails, something that had eluded him thus far. He began making notes on his phone with the name of the restaurant and the available dishes. We would soon be back, once he finished surveying the market and zeroed upon the stalls of his choice—wherever there's plenty of variety, his objective is to optimize the species he eats.

As we walked through the adjacent lanes, we spotted many different restaurants—Malaysian, Thai and even an Indian restaurant. Some were letting their cooking demos advertise their food, while others were advertising their wares by shouting out their specialties. One particularly pushy vendor tried hard to convince me that I must taste his bun cha. Bun cha, a Vietnamese dish made of grilled pork and rice noodles, is supposed to have originated in Hanoi. The dish became world famous after Barack Obama had dinner at a local bun cha restaurant with Anthony Bourdain. The vendor tried to convince me that his was the very same restaurant by pointing at a giant photo of Obama and Bourdain plastered on the wall. I had to tell him that while I didn't eat pork, I am sufficiently up to date with pop culture and I knew that the Obama bun cha restaurant is in Hanoi. He was extremely persistent and continued to insist that he was the creator of the presidential dish even as we walked away. I marvelled at his ability to craft such an in-depth sales pitch.

Right next to this, we found a stall selling banh mi, the Vietnamese sandwich made of vegetables, sauce and barbecued pork. Since banh mi is one of the most quintessential Vietnamese dishes, Vivek decided to get one. At this point, we'd seen most of the stalls, so I decided to order the Vietnamese pizza and the bamboo chicken from the first stall we had spotted.

Meanwhile, Vivek went to order the snails. He now noticed that the stall also sold crayfish. He thought about it and decided to get the crayfish first and go back for the snails if he was still hungry. Crayfish, unlike their name, are not really fish but crustaceans that are part of the lobster species found in freshwater. He stopped to watch the cooking process as well.

I found him at this stall just in time to see the chef dip his hand into an aquarium that contained half a dozen crayfish. Each crayfish was about six inches long with eight-inch-long, thin claws. Vivek pointed at the one he wanted and the chef took it out. I expected that the crayfish would be butchered before it was cooked and wondered if I should look away. To my horror, the chef instead pushed a skewer through the body of the still live crayfish. Then, he placed it onto a grill with hot coals directly under it. I saw it twitch for a while and wondered if Vivek was okay with this or if he was as horror-struck as I was.

'That's inhuman,' I exclaimed, once I collected my wits.

'Don't worry,' Vivek said. 'Many cultures believe that crayfish, like lobsters and other crustaceans, don't feel any pain. That's why they're cooked alive.'

'I don't know how we can judge that,' I replied.

'Even if we don't know for sure about pain, we do know that certain crustaceans have bacteria in their bodies that grow as soon as they die, so they need to be cooked alive to ensure the bacteria are destroyed,' he informed me. That seemed to make more sense than trying to play God and determine whether or not a lobster could feel pain.

Vivek also asked me to order a banh mi while the crayfish was cooking so I walked away to place that order. Every stall gave us an order number. We needed to find a table and place the number next to us. That way, the servers would know to drop off the dishes at our table. Since the front area opened out into the streets and was cooler, I found a seat there. Soon, Vivek joined me and we waited for the food to arrive.

The banh mi was the first to arrive. Banh mi is made in many different ways across Vietnam—some sandwiches are made with a pate, while others are made with barbecued pork. The sauces are also different at different stalls, so it makes sense to eat banh mi in as many different places as possible. The banh mi was well marinated and had a sublime blend of barbecued pork with the bite of fresh vegetables and sauces. We later tried asking the stall owner which sauce he used, but all he would tell us was that this was a family recipe.

The next dish to arrive was the Vietnamese pizza. I later discovered that this dish is sold on street corners across Vietnam and it quickly became one of my go-to snacks. I really like thin crust pizzas and this base was very similar, just that it was cooked over a grill instead of being wood fired resulting in the papad-like texture. The pizza was topped with a mix of hot and sweet sauces, a quail egg and some vegetables. Like any other street-side snack, it's easy to get it customized to your tastes and preferences.

The crayfish arrived last. Vivek was very happy with his decision once he tasted it. It was well grilled and came with a side of Vietnamese chilli sauce and lemon. Crayfish meat is similar to other crustaceans like shrimp and lobster, but it's much juicier and tastier than either of those.

Crayfish: Vivek's first cooked alive dish

Once we were done with these, we were pretty full. Or, at least, I was. Vivek decided to head back to get the snails. The shop was like snail heaven since it contained many snail and clam varieties. Vivek ordered two kinds—a sea snail and a plate of finger snails. He was fairly certain that the 'finger snails' were actually razor clams. As an added bonus, he stopped by the stall with the bamboo chicken and ordered that as well.

The sea snail was large and oyster-like in its appearance. It was grilled with chili and salt to taste. The finger snails were smaller and cooked in a butter-garlic sauce. Most of the weird foods we've come across in our travels are typically fried, possibly in an attempt to mask the natural taste of the unfamiliar food. The snails were an exception. They looked and smelled delicious and Vivek confirmed that they tasted exceptional.

A group of Indian men on a table to our left seemed to agree with my assessment on the appearance and aroma of the snails. They hesitantly asked us which stall we'd bought the food from while pointing at the finger snails. Vivek was thrilled to find fellow bizarre-food connoisseurs and gave them detailed directions to the stall. That was when one of them had the foresight to ask him what he was eating. He happily told them they were both snails and described the differences between them as I watched their faces fall.

Five minutes later, they were tucking into some khichdi sourced from Sher-e-Punjab, the Indian restaurant in the market. Vivek finished his snails, though he was quite disheartened that he hadn't converted our Indian friends to try something new.

He then went on to consume the bamboo chicken, a dish of grilled marinated chicken inside a hollowed-out bamboo. It was definitely a popular dish—I could spot both the chicken and pork versions at many other tables. The chicken was well marinated and very flavourful. As it had been cooked in the bamboo, it had an added flavour from the bamboo.

After this snack, he was also full so we decided to call it a night. In a single day, Vietnam had lived up to its reputation of being a haven for foodies. As he updated his chart, I realized that this was an evening where he had eaten multiple new species. It was in close competition with his bug-cart experience for the most enriching evening meal.

On days like this, Vivek sleeps peacefully with the knowledge that he has made a quantum leap in food explorations.

Ben Thanh Street Food Market, 26–28–30 Thủ Khoa Huân, Phường Bến Thành					
Item	Banh Mi	Vietnamese Pizza with Quail Eggs	Grilled Crayfish	Sea Snail, Finger Snail	Bamboo Chicken
Taste	★★★★	★★★★★	★★★★★	★★★★★	★★★★★
Price	₫35,000	₫55,000	₫85,000	₫150,000	₫75,000
Fear Factor	2	2	3	3	1
New Species	None	None	Crayfish	Sea Snail, Finger Snail	None

An Ardent Cricket Fan

Ho Chi Minh City is the site of the Vietnam War or the American War, depending on which side you take. In order to combat the better-prepared forces of the Americans and the South Vietnamese forces during the war, communist guerrilla troops of the Viet Cong dug thousands of miles of tunnels, including the extensive network of tunnels that lies under Cu Chi, northwest of Ho Chi Minh City. At the peak of the war, these tunnels linked Viet Cong support bases over a distance of 250 km, from Saigon all the way to the Cambodian border. Over time, there were guerrilla fighters who lived underground for years and the tunnels formed an extensive, multi-level network of homes, kitchens, hospitals and more. Essentially, an entire village evolved underground.[27]

Like many other visitors to Vietnam, we went on a tour to Cu Chi, where we learned the history behind the tunnels, saw the booby traps the fighters built for the American forces and were even able to walk through a portion of the tunnels. After about ten minutes and forty metres of a claustrophobic squat through the narrow pathways, we developed a renewed respect for the Vietnamese people who were able to live their lives there. The Cu Chi tour is an eye-opener, showcasing the ingenuity of the people here. For those who are so inclined, there's also a shooting range in the premises where you can have your pick of guns from an MI6 to an AK47 and run through a round of bullets.

~

On the way back from the Cu Chi tour, we stopped at a local village that specialized in rice paper. Rice paper is a popular ingredient and is used to make rolls in Vietnam. The process of making rice paper is somewhat similar to dosas. The batter is much thinner and more watery and is made of a mix of rice flour, tapioca flour, salt and water. The glutinous nature of the rice paper comes from tapioca. It's spread out on a hot pan and covered so it's steam cooked. It is then removed and laid out on a bamboo plate to dry.

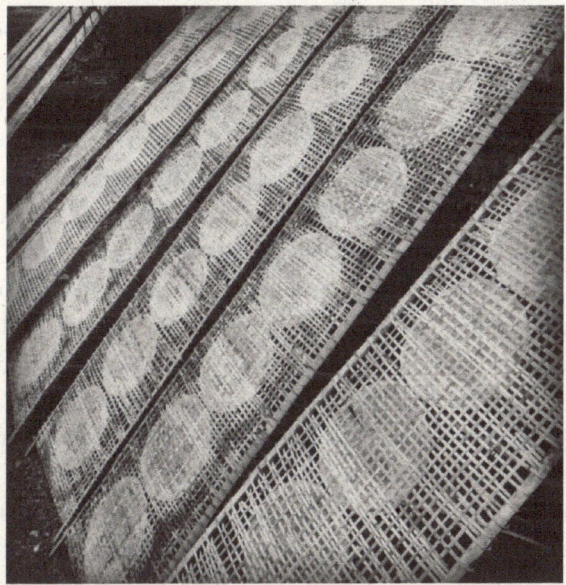

Making rice paper

We watched a demonstration of the process and were then allowed to attempt it ourselves. I made a hash of my attempt, primarily because I was unable to grasp the right technique to take it off the pan. I claimed that this was because it was similar to the first dosa off the *kallu*,* which almost always disintegrates, neglecting the fact that our host had been making rice paper all morning. Vivek was a natural and earned high praise. If the host is to be believed, he has an alternate career in rice paper making.

Once we learned to make rice paper, we were taken to our next stop, where we learned to make summer rolls using the rice paper. However, these were no ordinary summer rolls. The key ingredients were the crickets raised at the cricket farm that was to be our next stop. While crickets have been identified as a great source of protein and are becoming popular in the West, they have long been a staple food in Southeast Asia. They're also very easy to farm.

The cricket farm consisted of large troughs of plant waste, which served as cricket feed. Each trough had crickets in different life stages, ranging from eggs to those that were laying eggs, to larger ones ready to be harvested. Since the crickets are co-located with their feed, they overeat and are too fat to fly high. Therefore, they can't escape the height of the troughs. The farm owner also had a secondary business raising lizards, which are the natural predators of crickets. Excess crickets were used as feed for the lizards, which are also eaten across the region. The farm was a self-sufficient ecosystem in itself.

Once we finished walking around the farm, we were treated to tea and cricket rolls, that we had to make ourselves. We were seated at a long table, with a giant bowl of salad veggies (cucumbers, carrots and lettuce), crickets roasted

---

* Tamil word for the cast iron pan

in a lemony butter-garlic sauce and rice paper. Our guide demonstrated the method to make a Vietnamese summer roll.

Farm-to-table at the cricket farm

I made mine without the crickets and proved my lack of culinary skills yet again as I forgot to fold the rice paper before making the roll. I ended up with a giant mealy roll, instead of the tiny tasty rolls that we were supposed to make. Vivek started by eating the crickets in a summer roll but soon graduated to eating the crickets straight from the dish. He enjoyed the lemon-butter-garlic sauce that they were cooked in. The sauce turned out to be a staple for many Vietnamese dishes and was packed with flavour.

Cricket Farm, Cu Chi	
Item	*Cricket Spring Rolls*
Taste	★★★★★
Price	Part of a guided tour, but priceless
Fear Factor	5
New Species	Crickets

~

On our way back from the cricket farm, we were in for another treat. Our minivan stopped at a roadside juice shop. Our guide highly recommended the durian sugar cane juice as a refreshment. We have come across durian multiple times in many markets but always resisted it because of the smell. This time, I decided to join Vivek in the quest to eat adventurously by getting myself a glass of the juice.

Unlike the fruit, the juice didn't have a strong smell, probably because the sugar cane was able to mask it. The juice was creamy, sweet and very refreshing.

Vivek may have eaten many bizarre foods through our travels, but this juice was special because it marked my own attempt at trying something outside of my comfort zone! I had gotten over my fear of having the terribly stinky fruit right under my nose.

Roadside Juice stall, Cu Chi	
Item	*Durian and Sugar Cane Juice*
Taste	★★★★★
Price	₫50,000
Fear Factor	2
New Species	Durian

Recipe: Cricket Spring Roll

Ingredients
Roasted crickets in lemon–garlic sauce
Chopped vegetables: lettuce, cucumbers and carrots
Rice paper
Lemon, salt, pepper and chilli sauce to taste

Method

Dip the rice paper in water to soften it. Fold it in half, into a
    crescent shape. Lay it on a plate. Top with the vegetables
    and crickets.

Roll the paper into a cylinder, while ensuring that the stuffing
    doesn't fall out.

Enjoy!

It Quacks like a Duck

A trip to Vietnam is incomplete without a trip to the Mekong Delta. The Delta, also known as the Nine Dragon River Delta because its formed by nine rivers, lies to the west of Ho Chi Minh City. The Mekong Delta is one of the most fertile regions in the land and is called the Rice Bowl of Vietnam. The Delta is triangle-shaped stretching from My Tho in the East to Chau Doc and Ha Thien in the North West, down to Ca Mau. The Delta is like a water world where boats, houses and markets float upon numerous rivers, canals and streams that crisscross over the landscape.[28]

We went on a speedboat to the Can Giouc Market, near the mangrove forests of Can Gio. The riverside market was bustling with energy early in the morning. This was a rural market, very different from the city-markets we had seen elsewhere in Southeast Asia. A stroll through the market gave us a glimpse into rural life on the Mekong Delta. Everywhere we looked we could see roadside vendors selling fresh vegetables, meat and fish. We even spotted a stall selling ducklings for purchase. The ducklings were housed in crates by the road. They were sitting in an orderly fashion in their crates. We watched while a customer stopped by and purchased a dozen ducklings. The ducklings were packed into a polythene bag with a cardboard bottom, to add stability and to help avoid squishing the ducklings. I wondered why anyone would need a dozen ducklings and what kind of dish would be made from them when Vivek told me that the customer would likely raise the poultry.

Right next to this, a lady was sitting by the road. She had an orderly line up of ducks and geese perched on bamboo slats in front of her. I thought that these too were for rearing before I spotted the weighing scale placed by her side. Our guide confirmed my suspicions that these were for consumption. He told me that customers would point at the bird they wanted and she would kill it, skin it and sell it right there. If we waited by the side for a while, we would've probably been able to see one of her transactions, but we moved ahead.

Disciplined merchandise: Ducks and geese for sale

As we moved through the market, we passed by the seafood section, which also had stalls selling varied fishing gear. We saw many different types of frogs, fish and shellfish being sold in these stalls.

I suddenly spotted a mudskipper that had managed to crawl out of its basket and was now crossing the road. Mudskippers are fantastical amphibious fish that can survive on land. They can travel distances, feed themselves and spend a large part of their day on land and even more in mud. I wondered if we should point out the renegade mudskipper to the vendor, but decided to keep mum.

We allowed it to enjoy its *Shawshank Redemption* moment and escape into the by-lanes of the market. We believe that the mudskipper went on an adventure and managed to make it back home to the river.

~

Later that night, we decided to explore the Ben Thanh Night Market. It was quaint with multiple stalls selling things we hadn't seen anywhere else. There were many stalls dedicated to selling weasel coffee, a specialty of Vietnam. Weasel coffee is made from the dung of the civet cat. The civet cat, a relative of the mongoose, is native to Southeast Asian jungles. Sometime after the French colonists introduced the country to Robusta beans, coffee growers discovered that beans eaten and excreted by civets produced a more mellow drink than those harvested from the fields.[29] We didn't manage to muster up the courage to taste some, given the rich backstory.

There were many seafood stalls which had aquarium-like displays of their wares placed right in front of the barbecue grills where these would be cooked. In one of these stalls, we even saw a large turtle in a tub, right next to the usual suspects like prawns, crabs and clams of all sizes. The stall owner tried convincing us that this would be the perfect dish for a romantic dinner date at his stall! He quoted a reasonable sum of đ1.5 Million (approx. Rs 4,000) for the turtle. While Vivek has eaten turtles at that price point before, he knew he was likely to find a different species awaiting him elsewhere in the market and suggested that we move forward.

We also walked through the two lanes with all the fashion and souvenir shops without buying anything. This walk was enough for Vivek to drum up an appetite and peruse all the menus in depth. Most food stalls had the regulars like fried rice, fried noodles and banh mi. And then Vivek spotted 'the one'—mudskippers. Notwithstanding the fact that he helped me aid the escape of this very creature earlier the same day, he decided to have mudskippers for dinner.

I got myself a plate of fried rice while we waited for his dish, braised mudskipper served with steamed rice. As soon as the dish arrived in a heady aroma of spices, I knew Vivek would enjoy it.

The Vietnamese palate is a lot like the Indian one. The mudskipper was relatively boneless and the only bones were along the long, central spine. Vivek figured out that the most efficient way to eat it was to hold it on one end with his teeth and pull off all the meat around the spine in one go. Clearly, the time spent in eating *murungakka sambhar** had helped him perfect this technique!

---

* Drumstick sambhar

Mudskipper

Vivek confirmed that the mudskipper was spicy and well cooked, the perfect choice for a romantic dinner. I was busy philosophizing about how we had completed a karmic cycle, by eating mudskippers after letting one escape this very fate.

Food Stall, Ben Thanh Night Market	
Item	*Street Style Mudskipper and Rice*
Taste	★★★★★
Price	₫100,000
Fear Factor	2
New Species	Mudskipper

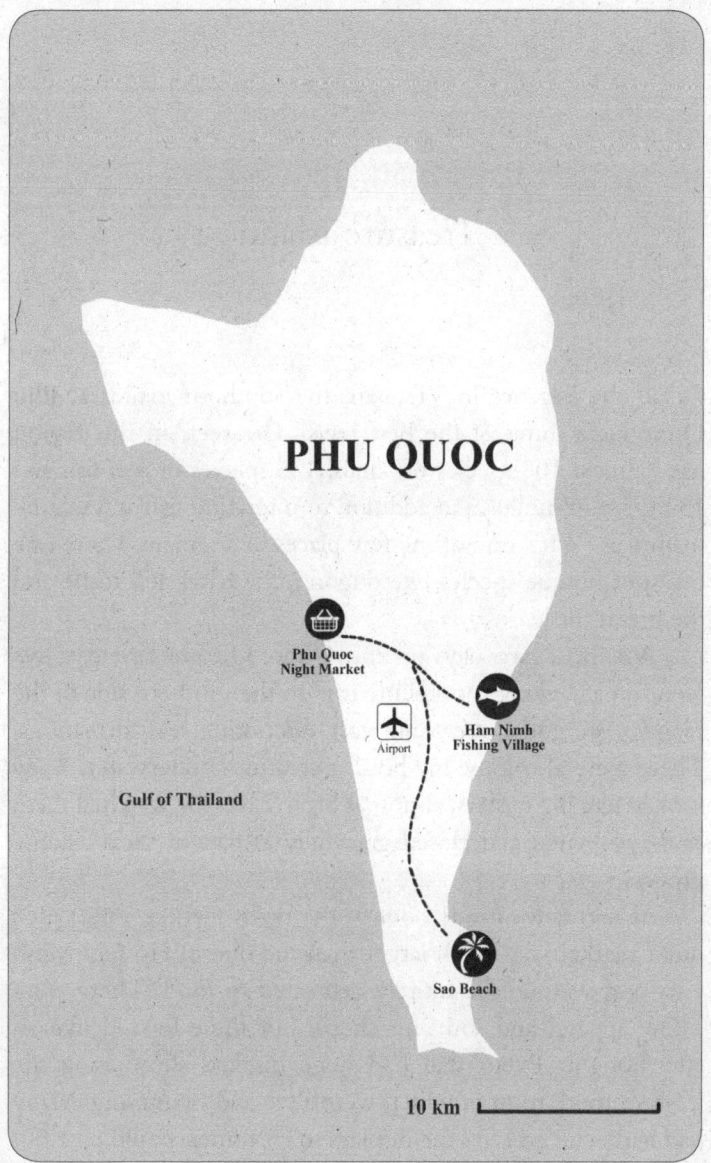

Treasure Island

Of all the beaches in Vietnam, the southern islands at Phu Quoc have some of the best reefs. The reefs in this region have almost 108 species of corals, 135 species of reef fish and 132 types of molluscs in addition to migrating fish and marine mammals.[30] It's one of the few places in Vietnam where one can spot unique species like dugong, the hawksbill turtle and the green turtle.

We spent two days in Phu Quoc. On our first day, we went on a daylong snorkelling trip on the southern side of the islands. We got to see some very interesting reef formations. There were also some big bivalve creatures underwater. They looked like big oysters, almost as big as cars. We watched them as they opened and closed gracefully as part of their feeding process.

At night, we headed out to the night market. Phu Quoc night market was much larger than the one in Ho Chi Minh City and was almost entirely dedicated to food. There were a few apparel and souvenir shops, but these looked like an afterthought. Every stall had huge displays showcasing the fresh seafood, most of which were alive and swimming. Many had barbecue grills by the displays so customers could pick out what they wanted and have it cooked right in front of them.

This was Vivek's dream market. Newer varieties of snail and snake were on his radar.

As we walked through the market, I felt like I was walking through an aquarium, thanks to the size and variety of the displays. Vivek examined the quality of the wares at every stall and did price comparisons. As he evaluated his choices, I wandered around trying to decide if I should get some Vietnamese pizza for a snack or if I should wait till he decided where he would eat, so I could also order at the same place. Suddenly, a woman walked up to one of the stalls and began quizzing the owner.

'What is this,' she asked pointing at a tank with something that looked like the puffer balls we used to get as kids.

'That's a sea urchin,' the owner replied.

I remembered that Vivek had tried sea urchin sushi in Seattle and liked it. I was about to call him to check this display out when she asked her next question.

'What about that,' she said, pointing at another tank.

'That's a snail,' said the owner.

'But, it's huge! It looks like a conch,' she exclaimed.

'Yes, it's an elephant snail. Weighs about a kilogram,' he said.

She seemed interested in the conch and asked for the price. The owner looked thrilled and told her it cost ₫200,000. She kept staring at it.

Then the owner said, 'Madam, do you want to buy it? We can barbecue it with garlic-butter, or lemongrass, or Thai-peanut sauce.'

'Oh no, I'm vegetarian. I was just curious,' she replied and walked off leaving him staring at her in shock.

I had the urge to tell her that if she was so curious about the molluscs found in the oceans near Phu Quoc she should go on a snorkelling trip!

Just then, Vivek called out to show me that he'd found snakes and he was getting one barbecued. While he had eaten smaller snakes before, this was the first time he was eating a large snake. It was about two feet in length, fat and fleshy. The snakes were all swimming in an enclosure—fat snakes, grey snakes, green snakes, black snakes with stripes. Some were swimming, some lying at the bottom of the container. Snakes that would make you run like Usain Bolt if you ever met them in your garden or elsewhere. It was like the snake park at a zoo. Except, here you could point at one and it would be cooked for you. Which is what Vivek did.

The owner immediately scooped up his chosen snake using a net. Vivek was so excited that he went back into the kitchen to see how the snake was cleaned. He soon emerged as they were bringing out a now headless snake and placing it on the grill outside the stall.

He came and sat down at the table for a few minutes, looking very shaken.

'What happened,' I asked.

'I can't tell you what happened inside the kitchen,' he said, as he walked back to the grill. I later discovered that the snake had been cooked in a manner identical to that of the crayfish—cooked alive.

Vivek started taking pictures of his snake on the grill. A crowd gathered by the barbecue grill as passers-by realized that a snake was on it. People started laughing nervously, taking photographs and looking around to pinpoint who had the courage to order this. Vivek moved away from the snake and pretended to be another shocked spectator. I couldn't stop laughing at the sight of tourists trying to guess who in their sane minds could have purchased the snake without realizing that the purchaser was in their midst. Once the barbecue was done, the whole snake was served on a plate. After giving us a few minutes for photo ops, the server cut it into smaller pieces with a giant pair of scissors.

Snake on the grill

'Doesn't it look like she's cutting the ribbons for an inauguration,' Vivek said excitedly. 'This is an inauguration into a new bizarre eating experience for me!'

'So, how does snake taste,' I asked.

'Brilliant! The skin is thick and similar to fish skin—it's stretchy and salty. The meat is smooth and quite tasty.'

Food Stall, Phu Quoc Night Market	
Item	*Subsessor Snake*
Taste	★★★★★
Price	₫450,000
Fear Factor	5
New Species	Water Snake

~

For dessert, I suggested roll-up ice cream. It was similar to the stone mix ice cream you see elsewhere, where the ice cream is mixed with fruit and other toppings on a stone slab. In this case, it's almost a stir-fried ice cream, where milk is poured onto the chilled slab and mixed with the toppings. As the chopping happens, milk begins to crystallize and sets into ice cream. For the finale, the ice cream is rolled into a flower-like shape so you get a cup with an ice cream flower. It reminded me of how the Parisian gelato shops served their gelato in a cone. I'm not much of an ice cream person, but the Vietnamese roll-up ice cream is now one of my favourites.

After dessert, we went on another walk through the market because Vivek said the snake wasn't enough to be a complete meal. Or maybe, Vivek had seen more species during our initial walk and didn't want to miss out. As I suspected, it was the latter. He had been eyeing the sea urchin. I suggested we walk back to the stall where the curious vegetarian had done her research since she had gotten the vendor's hopes up. While we ordered the sea urchin, Vivek was tempted by a giant conch-shaped snail. He's always intrigued by the conches that are blown during ceremonies and wanted to know what the animal inside it looked and tasted like.

We were walking back to the tables when we passed by a stall that appeared to be selling tiny crabs. Or that's what Vivek thought the first few times he'd walked by it and ignored it. However, this time around, he decided to give the small crabs a closer look. Up close, he realized he had chanced upon the rarest species on his list, sea cicada. All his research had indicated that the only place to find sea cicadas was an island in Thailand. Yet, here they were staring him in the face. And so, he got a plate of that as well.

Sea cicadas. Also called sand crabs, mole crabs or sand fleas

Sea cicadas are like mini crabs, except they're shaped more like a beetle than a crab. They're so small that the shell is soft and chewable, each of them is the size of a peanut. Vivek started snacking on them as if they were peanuts, only to realize that these were deep fried and were too heavy for him to finish a plate of by himself. He ate most of it but wished he had not ordered so much out of greed. They taste like shrimp, but since you're also eating the shell, it's more like eating a shrimp with its tail.

I was curious to see how the sea urchin would be served since it's essentially a ball with spikes all around it. The top was cut off and used as a bowl in which the meat was served. It looked like the bread bowls in which clam chowder is served.

The meat inside the conch had been cut into pieces, cooked and then laid back in beautifully.

Grilled conch

It was served with a garlic-butter sauce and a few sprigs of lemongrass. Vivek is now a big fan of the garlic sauce in Vietnam and wants to make some at home.

Vietnam certainly lived up to its reputation for bizarre foods. Until we got to Phu Quoc, the Ben Thanh Night Market was the place that allowed us to add most species to a chart in a single night. Phu Quoc topped that and how! Vivek's big win that night was the sea cicada.

Little did he know what awaited him.

Food Stall, Phu Quoc Night Market			
Item	*Sea Urchin*	*Conch*	*Grilled Sea Cicadas*
Taste	★★★★	★★★★	★★★
Price	₫100,000	₫200,000	₫200,000
Fear Factor	4	4	5
New Species	Sea Urchin	Conch Snail	Sea Cicadas

~

The next day, we rented a bike to go around the island. We started by heading to Sao Beach. It was exactly as I'd imagined—white sands and clear water. There were swings hanging off palm trees by the ocean. You can swing while dipping your toes in the ocean. We spent the morning relaxing at the beach.

Our next stop was the Ham Ninh fishing village. We barely exited the parking lot in the village when we spotted a street-side shop selling seahorses. Seahorses, which are extremely hard to catch, are a specialty of Phu Quoc island. At Ham Nimh, they make a wine out of seahorses and rice, which is rumoured to treat fertility issues. Vivek was thrilled to stumble upon seahorses since he knew this was a once-in-a-lifetime opportunity. It was unlikely that we would find them in Hanoi since we hadn't seen them in Ho Chi Minh City. Seahorses are also terribly rare and not available in most countries. Vivek couldn't control his excitement while all I could think of was how cute they looked.

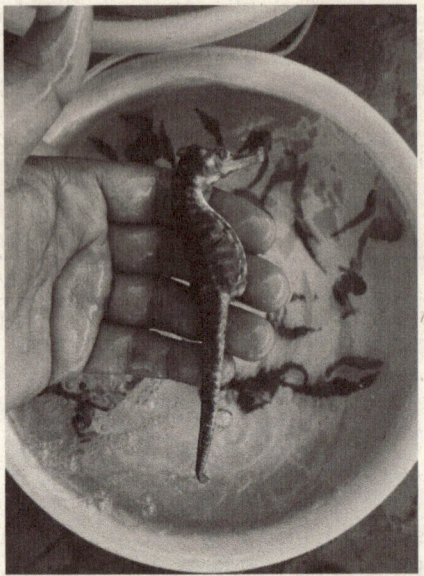

Seahorse at Ham Nimh Fishing Village

The two stalls here were selling live and dried seahorses out of baskets on the side of the road. Vivek hoped that one of the restaurants on the pier would have the dish on their menu. The pier and the restaurants there were on stilts somewhat like the floating village we had previously visited. In some ways, the feeling of sitting at a table here was very similar to that at the floating markets since you could feel the water move under your feet.

We soon realized we had only one choice of restaurant—the one with an English menu. Their menu didn't have any exotic species. We had to make do with fried rice and since we were in a fishing village Vivek also ordered the fresh oysters. Oysters are a popular delicacy across the world, though many people don't realize that raw oysters are alive. Just like the crayfish, raw oysters are also unsafe for consumption once they are dead because of the bacteria they harbour. The oysters at Ham Nimh were very fresh and directly from the source. It was so direct, we could see the catch brought in as we ate.

Food Stall, Ham Nimh Fishing Village Pier	
Item	*Oysters*
Taste	★★★
Price	₫150,000
Fear Factor	3
New Species	Oysters

~

After lunch, we made a pit stop at the stall with the seahorses on our way back. He now bargained with the seller to convince a nearby restaurant to cook the seahorse so he could finally eat it.

Seahorse turned out to be another expensive dish by Vietnamese standards, costing ₫500,000. Vivek was excited because of the rarity of the dish. The skin was like an edible groundnut shell, hard and with a scaly texture. The meat inside is semi-solid with no bones. As he ate it, the cook also came up to tell him that he could eat the entire thing, including the head, which he did.

I realized that seahorses looked just as cute on a plate as they did swimming around. I had to make my peace with the fact that these were martyred due to Vivek's quest to eat his way through the world.

'Of all the things I've eaten, this is the most heartless,' said Vivek as he agreed with me, 'But also the rarest!'

Fried seahorse

Food Stall, Ham Nimh Fishing Village	
Item	*Fried Seahorse*
Taste	★★★
Price	₫400,000
Fear Factor	5
New Species	Seahorse

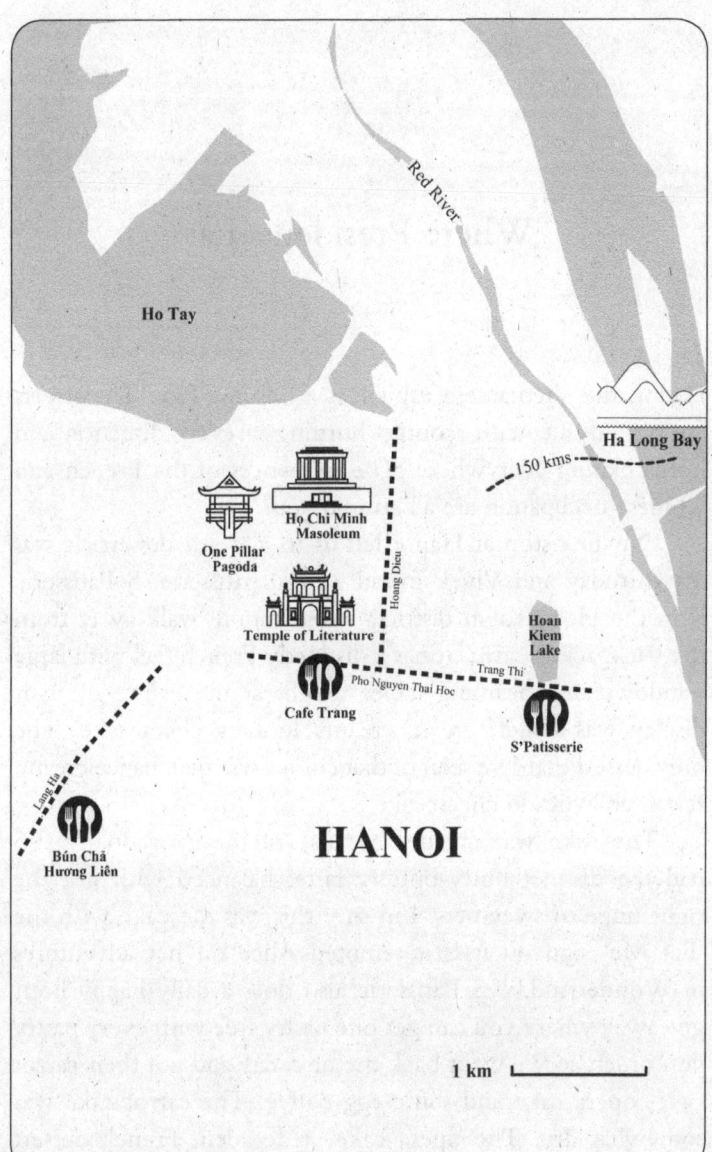

Red River

Ho Tay

Ha Long Bay

150 kms

One Pillar
Pagoda

Ho Chi Minh
Masoleum

Hoang Dieu

Temple of Literature

Hoan
Kiem
Lake

Trang Thi

Pho Nguyen Thai Hoc

Cafe Trang

S'Patisserie

Lang Ha

Bún Chá
Hương Liên

HANOI

1 km

Where Presidents Eat

Hanoi, the Vietnamese capital, is a bustling city. The streets are brightly lit, with scooters hurtling in every direction and horns blaring everywhere. The influences of the French and Chinese occupation are all around you.

Our first stop at Hanoi led us to a weird dessert. It was my birthday and Vivek found a local patisserie. S Patisserie is in the Hoan Kiem district, a ten-minute walk away from the backpackers' area. It has a distinctly French feel with large windows and gleaming tables. Right at the centre of their display was a light green, creamy looking cheesecake. The only dessert that I've seen of that colour was matcha ice cream. It was an avocado cheesecake.

The cake was creamy because of the avocado. It also had the distinct nutty-buttery taste, balanced with just the right tinge of sweetness. I'm sure this was the cake with the 'Eat Me' sign on it that tempted Alice on her adventures in Wonderland.[31] S Patisserie also does a daily happy hour giveaway where you can get one pastry free with every pastry you order, so we went back the next day and got their carrot cake, opera cake and some egg coffee. The carrot cake was somewhat dry. The opera cake, a decadent French dessert which combines chocolate and coffee, was very well made and would transport you to Paris if you just closed your eyes. Egg coffee sounds weird but is actually quite tasty. The coffee is smoother and creamier than regular coffee because it has egg whites whipped into it. We had it here, as well as at Note Café—a quirky cafe that lets you write notes and stick them on the walls.

However, if I go back, it will only be for the avocado cake.

S Patisserie, 17 Hang Khay Street, Hoan Kiem District				
Item	Avocado Cake	Carrot Cake	Opera Cake	Egg Coffee
Taste	★★★★	★★★	★★★★★	★★★★★
Price	₫50,000	~₫50,000	~₫50,000	₫55,000
Fear Factor	2	1	1	2
New Species	None	None	None	None

~

We started our explorations at Hanoi by visiting the Ho Chi Minh Mausoleum. In addition to the remains of Ho Chi Minh, the complex also houses the one-pillar pagoda, built by the Emperor Ly Thai Tong in 1049. One night, the childless emperor dreamt of a private audience with the Buddha, who was holding a baby. The Buddha was seated on a lotus flower, in a lotus-shaped pond and gave the king the baby. A month later the queen was pregnant and later gave birth to a baby boy. To repay the gift from the Buddha, the pagoda was constructed, with a single pillar, so it was reminiscent of the lotus seat on which the Buddha sat. The original pagoda was destroyed by the French in 1954 and was refurbished by the Vietnamese government in 1955.[32]

This is the most interesting pagoda. It's situated in the centre of a small lake and looks like a flower that's blooming right out of the water. The single pillar is the stalk and the ornate roof is lotus-shaped. The pagoda is thronged with locals who believe that a visit here has miraculous powers of fertility.

We then went to the Temple of Literature, one of the best-preserved examples of Vietnamese architecture. This is the site of Vietnam's first national university. The university consists of small buildings surrounded by five walled courtyards. The walls cut out all the ambient noise, making this an oasis of calm in the centre of the bustling city. The first two courtyards are filled with beautiful gardens housing ancient trees, lotus ponds and topiary animal sculptures. The third courtyard is known as Thien Quang Thinh or the Wall of Clarity. The fourth courtyard features the House of Ceremonies and a sanctuary of Confucius. The House of Ceremonies is a hall with red columns and wood beam ceilings that have ancient lanterns hanging from them. It's easily one of the most beautiful parts of the temple.[33]

It took us an hour to walk through the temple. We then took a break for lunch. As we walked around the area, we spotted Café Trang, a coffee shop advertising Mantis Shrimp Pho. I pointed it out to Vivek, who missed eating mantis shrimp in Phu Quoc because he was too full. Mantis shrimp, also called *tom tit*, is a long, translucent shrimp. Imagine a shrimp version of a centipede. The Vietnamese use this because of the crunchy and chewy meat. They're strong and the most important predators in their habitats.

Vivek's reaction to the soup was a testament to the taste of the mantis shrimp. He doesn't like noodle soups yet he gulped down this in minutes. The soup broth was very mildly flavoured and did not overpower the taste of the shrimp.

Mantis shrimp: The superman of the sea

The mild sweetness of shrimp was well complemented by the lemongrass and herbs flavouring the soup. Once we were done with lunch, we were ready to head out to our next stop, the Hanoi Hilton.

Café Trang, 47 Ngo Tat To, Quan Dong Da	
Item	*Mantis Shrimp Pho*
Taste	★★★★★
Price	đ100,000
Fear Factor	3
New Species	Mantis Shrimp

~

The 'Hanoi Hilton' is the ironic name given to the Hoa Lao prison used by the French colonists for political prisoners and later by the North Vietnamese for United States Prisoners of War. The prison museum recreates the prison experience, including the ways in which the Vietnamese revolutionaries were confined by the French in the earlier part of the twentieth century.[34] The prison evokes a wide variety of emotions ranging from sorrow to disgust and even anger, depending on your politics. It was an overwhelming experience so we headed out to walk around the Hoan Kiem Lake while we mulled over it.

That night, we decided to head to Bun Cha Huon Lieng, also known as 'Obama' Bun Cha because they hosted Barack Obama, the then-President of the USA in 2016.[35] The restaurant is tucked away in an unassuming street in the French Quarter of Hanoi. Inside, it's very functional with long, communal tables where people sit down, place their orders, eat and leave. It's like the Vietnamese version of a Sangeetha or a Saravana Bhavan. The only additions to the ambience are photos of Obama and Bourdain, so you can see that your eating experience is identical to theirs.

Vivek had the 'Obama combo', a bowl of bun cha, deep fried fish rolls and Hanoi beer. Bun cha is a dish made of fatty, grilled pork with white rice noodles and herbs. It also comes with a dipping sauce made of fish sauce combined with sugar, lemon juice, vinegar, stock, crushed garlic and chilli. The sauce makes the sweet and sour soul of the dish. The herbs and rice noodles are served separately so patrons can mix them in preferred proportions. The herbs served include cabbage, basil, rice paddy herb (*ngo*) and beansprouts.

The bun cha was made with grilled pork, *char siew* and it was well cooked with some delicious charred portions. The dipping sauce was very tasty and had the right mix of sweet and spice.

A presidential meal

Anthony Bourdain often said that Vietnamese food was his favourite[36] and it's quite clear why he picked Bun Cha Huong Lien as the place to treat a President to dinner.

Bun Cha Huong Lien, 24 Le Van Huu	
Item	*Obama Combo*
Taste	★★★★★
Price	₫85,000
Fear Factor	2
New Species	None

Halong and Thanks for All the Fish!

Halong Bay is a UNESCO world heritage site in Vietnam that's often rated amongst the top natural wonders of the world. The bay features limestone pillars and tiny islets in various shapes and sizes. It's a natural wonder where you can see stalactites and stalagmites in the caves across the coves. I realized early on that trying to fit it in a one-day trip wouldn't work since it involves a four hour plus drive from Hanoi to the Quang Ninh province. We found an overnight cruise to give us time to go kayaking, as well as see the spectacular sunset and sunrise on the bay. When I started looking up tour itineraries for the cruise, I spotted something that I knew would make Vivek very happy.

'Did you know you can go squid fishing on Halong Bay,' I asked him.

'What?! Please tell me we booked the cruise that offers that,' he said.

'All of them offer it,' I assured him. 'It's an optional activity.'

'Fishing of any kind is never an optional activity,' he told me seriously.

I was glad that it was optional. I would watch and cheer while Vivek managed to catch a giant squid.

~

The first day on the cruise was packed with activities and heavy meals. We left Hanoi at 7 a.m. and reached the docks at noon. Lunch was a five-course meal that we ate on the two-hour journey from the village to Bai Tu Long Bay. The spread started with peanut salad and fried fish, followed by a main course of steamed rice, mango chicken, steamed vegetables and squid curry. After all that food, I was glad that dessert was a fruit salad, albeit with cream.

Once we were at Bai Tu Long Bay, we had about thirty minutes to relax after which there was a kayaking trip organized for us. When I first heard about the kayaking, I imagined that we would be given instructions on the basics. I was in for a rude shock. We were taken to the kayaks on a smaller boat. Once we got to the kayaks, we were asked to hop on and get ourselves to an island in the distance. The tour leader said that the water in the bay was so still it was impossible for anyone to have trouble. I was quite sure that I would be the exception and would topple over!

Vivek began giving me instructions. He was quite well-versed with the mechanics since he had been kayaking with Saurav at Vasind. Based on his confidence in his directions, it sounded like he knew what he was doing. However, despite his best efforts, I found it hard to find a rhythm. I was trying to figure out how to move the oar when I realized our group had Type A kayakers who were competing to reach the island first. My competitive spirit kicked in and I gave myself an upper body workout while trying to overtake them. We managed to move ahead of the last kayak, and I mentally congratulated myself on not being the last. Just as I was rejoicing at this thought, they passed us by, whooping gleefully. My efforts had done nothing except tire me out. I gave up and concentrated on trying to get to the island. Unfortunately, my attempts resulted in a lot of water sloshing into the boat. It's a solid testament to Vivek's ability to row that we managed to reach our destination.

Once you're at the cove, you can take a swim. We skipped the swim because it was cold and windy. Instead, we collected some unique shells, some of which looked like they had eyes because clams were growing on them. We then had to kayak back to our boat and this time I took the seat behind. This helped me watch and mimic Vivek's movements. I was finally able to contribute to the effort of getting back to the deck. We still came last so I don't plan to participate in any kayak races any time soon.

Once we were back on the cruise ship, it was time for dinner. This was an even more elaborate meal, with seven courses. Vivek suddenly found out that the crew had already begun squid fishing on the front deck. He immediately abandoned the dinner table. I was still stuffed from the elaborate lunch, so I decided to go out on the deck to watch the fishing.

Vivek was sitting outside on the deck with the crew. They were holding fishing lines with hooks at the end. Their method seemed pretty unscientific to me because they weren't using any bait. They dropped the fishing lines in the water and jerked them out with a flick of their wrists. Sometimes the hook came out clean and at other times, they caught a squid. We later discovered that this is, in fact, the real method for squid fishing, also called jigging. The squid gets attracted to the fly near the hook and they get hooked because of the flick.

I also spotted one of the crew fishing with a net instead of a line. He was hanging off the side of the boat with a net that he was submerging and pulling out of the water. He was using the lights of the boat to gauge the best spot to drop his net. Vivek was eyeing him and mentally evaluating if he could attempt this. I quickly reminded him that he doesn't know how to swim and I didn't want him to become the bait for a bigger fish. So, he borrowed a fishing line and attempted jigging instead.

I soon realized that watching other people fish isn't very interesting. It involves a lot of staring into the water. Post sunset, this means you're staring into space with very little light. I looked up at the night sky to see if I could spot some constellations to pass the time, but it wasn't a good night for stargazing either. I noticed many of the other guests wandering out and asking about the squid fishing. However, none of them attempted it. They were eager to head back in and continue with the seven-course dinner instead. I was impressed at Vivek's dedication, but that wasn't enough to keep me out in the cold for much longer. I went back into the dining area in time for the main course.

Catch of the day: Squid fishing at Halong Bay

Twenty minutes later, I was digging into a plate of fried rice when Vivek entered. In his hand was a plate with three grilled squids. He kept two for himself and shared one with our co-passengers who were sharing our table. Each squid was tiny, about the size of a finger. But Vivek was ecstatic at having caught and cooked something in the middle of the sea.

'This is the best squid I've ever eaten,' he said with a wide grin, as he is wont to do when he eats something that he's caught himself.

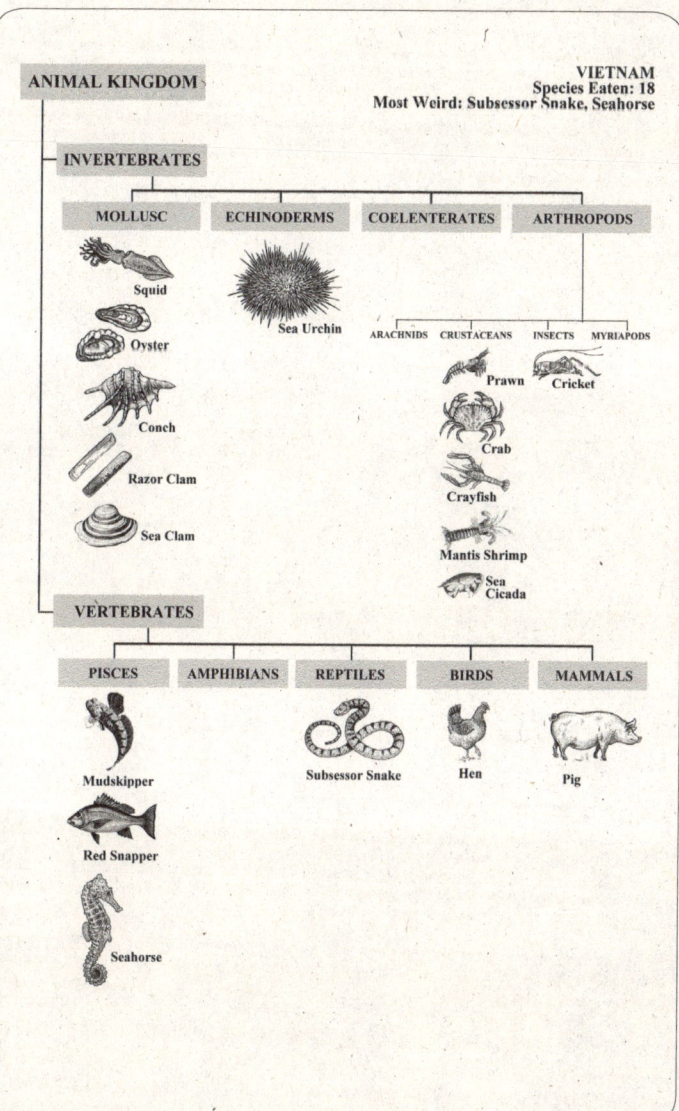

ANIMAL KINGDOM

VIETNAM
Species Eaten: 18
Most Weird: Subsessor Snake, Seahorse

INVERTEBRATES

MOLLUSC   ECHINODERMS   COELENTERATES   ARTHROPODS

Squid

Oyster

Sea Urchin

ARACHNIDS   CRUSTACEANS   INSECTS   MYRIAPODS

Conch

Prawn   Cricket

Razor Clam

Crab

Sea Clam

Crayfish

Mantis Shrimp

Sea Cicada

VERTEBRATES

PISCES   AMPHIBIANS   REPTILES   BIRDS   MAMMALS

Mudskipper

Subsessor Snake   Hen   Pig

Red Snapper

Seahorse

SINGAPORE

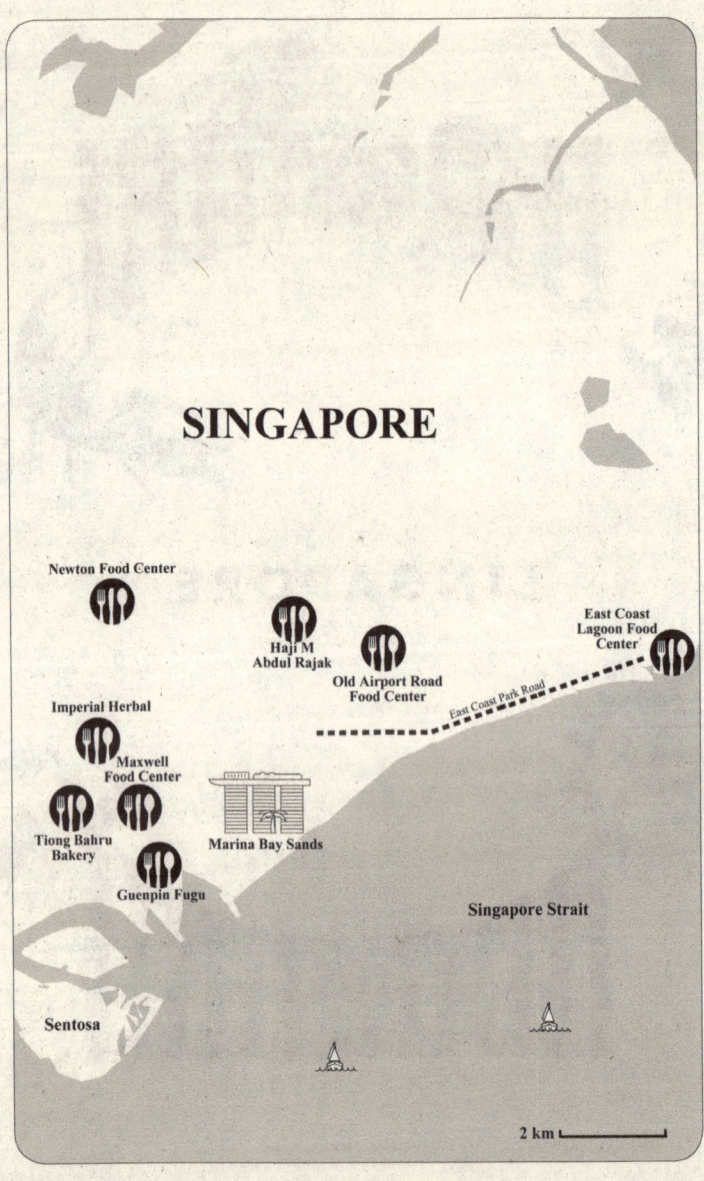

SINGAPORE

Newton Food Center

Haji M
Abdul Rajak

Old Airport Road
Food Center

East Coast
Lagoon Food
Center

Imperial Herbal

East Coast Park Road

Maxwell
Food Center

Tiong Bahru
Bakery

Marina Bay Sands

Guenpin Fugu

Singapore Strait

Sentosa

2 km

Right from the moment you get off the airplane into the world's top-rated airport, featuring manmade gardens and waterfalls that would rival some of the actual sights in many cities in the world, there's always something that can take your breath away in Singapore. Singapore is arguably the most well-planned city in the world. As we walked around in the rain, we saw how the roads were constructed in a way to ensure that rainwater was continuously drained.

Singapore has many tourist attractions catering to all types of travellers. You could take a cable car ride to Sentosa Island, a manmade island that houses many theme parks like Universal Studios, the Singapore Butterfly and Insect Kingdom and the Aquarium. Or, you could spend a day at the Gardens by the Bay, which features a temperature controlled garden housing plants from around the world. Children will love the bird shows and the variety of birds they can see at the Jurong Bird Park, as well as the night safari to see animals from around the world. For travellers who prefer going off the beaten path, there's the MacRitchie Reservoir where one can go on a treetop walk by hiking through a suspension bridge across the reservoir area. Or you could take a morbid tour through Haw Par Villa, the museum of death, which has a real-life depiction of the seven stages of hell as described in Chinese mythology.

But where Singapore really shines is the food. Singapore is a melting pot of culture, with cuisine that shows the influence of the native Malays as well as the Chinese, Indian, Peranakan,

Indonesian and Western traditions. The meals vary by budget, ranging from cheap hawker centres where you can have an entire meal for under SGD 5, to Michelin-starred restaurants with set menus, to hawker stalls that have earned Michelin stars. We picked Singapore to celebrate Vivek's thirty-fifth birthday in 2018 and see what new species it would add to the list.

A Tale of Tails and Webs

In Singapore, we were staying with our friends Anupam and Amita and their three-year-old twins Amay and Advay. The first thing Vivek told them was that he wanted to go to Imperial Herbal Restaurant, a restaurant that incorporates traditional herbal recipes with many 'unexpected' ingredients. It's a testament to their friendship that no eyebrows were raised. In fact, Anupam even offered to accompany us and show us around.

The restaurant is on the second floor of the Four Points by the Sheraton hotel and is very hard to miss when you exit the elevator. The entryway has a huge Chinese gong and is surrounded by glass cases that show off herbal remedies like snake, snake wine, crocodile meat, venison, different types of bones and more. The entrance houses a large aquarium that transports you to the night markets of Southeast Asia. The aquarium houses large fish, crabs, turtles and other sea creatures to pick from for your meal.

As soon as we were seated, Vivek started scanning the menu. Anupam recommended the signature dish, *Fu Rong* (Fluffy Egg White with Dried Scallops), as well as the Pumpkin Butter Prawns. They ordered the Braised Goose Web with Mushrooms and the Braised Crocodile Tail for the main course. We also added some egg-fried noodles to the order for me. Our server told us about the benefits of each dish. He took great pleasure in letting me know that both dishes were great for collagen production. Unfortunately, I had no plans to eat either just to look younger.

The Fu Rong, a remedy for good lung function, was first to arrive. It was exquisitely delicate, with a nest-like bed made of yam, topped with fluffy egg whites and dried scallops. The eggs were really light. Each bite of the dish had a balance of the light egg whites, with the crunch of the nest and some flavour from the scallops. It was worth going back for, many times over.

Pumpkin butter prawns

The next dish to arrive was the Pumpkin Butter Prawns. The sauce had a tinge of sweetness and included a generous helping of walnuts. While it was tasty, it couldn't compare to the Fu Rong.

Then came the two main courses, Braised Crocodile Tail and Braised Goose Web. At first, I was surprised to see the crocodile tail as I'd expected it to be the triangular-shaped end piece. However, this was a thick slab, likely from the centre of the tail.

The crocodile's tail

The thick skin covered some surprisingly soft and smooth meat inside that surrounded the weak reptilian bones. With many dishes, like fish, the skin had the flavour. The crocodile skin looked tough and was textured, however, Vivek and Anupam said that the dish was so well cooked the skin also tasted like meat. While the textured appearance made me think that I'd witness a Man vs Wild-type battle of knife and fork on the tail, the meat was coming off as smoothly as butter. The braising also helped retain its original flavour—while that could make it strong for many, Vivek loved it because he experienced the taste to the fullest.

I'd imagined that goose web would be something like the Bird's Nest, quite forgetting that only spiders weave webs. So I was quite startled when the dish arrived and I realized that the 'web' was the webbing from the feet.

Goose web

Vivek said that it tasted like the stronger version of a chicken's skin. Unlike chicken, it felt mealier in the mouth because it was larger and better developed. Vivek was unable to compare it to chicken feet because he hasn't tried that. However, he estimates that the goose web was much meatier because it needs to stretch to allow the bird to swim.

Imperial Restaurant, Four Points by Sheraton, Riverview				
Item	*Fu Rong*	*Pumpkin Butter Prawns*	*Braised Crocodile Tail*	*Braised Goose Web*
Taste	★★★★★	★★★	★★★★★	★★★★
Price	SGD5	SGD24	SGD16	SGD16
Fear Factor	2	2	5	5
New Species	Scallops	None	Crocodile Tail	Goose Web

~

After lunch, Anupam suggested a walk to the Tiong Bahru area so we could get pastries from the Tiong Bahru Bakery for dessert. We took a walk along the Singapore River through the Central Business District. We walked along the waterfront by some beautiful parks. Along the way, we passed by the Zion Hawker Centre, one of the many hawker centres in Singapore. There are over a hundred of them and each centre is located near a housing development to ensure that all citizens have access to hygienic food at affordable prices. Since it was late in the afternoon, many of the food stalls were shut. However, we were able to walk around and get a sense of the various cuisines available, ranging from the ubiquitous chilli crab and pepper crab to Peranakan dishes to local delicacies.

'This is such a fantastic concept,' exclaimed Vivek. 'Tomorrow onwards, we will eat four meals a day, each at a different hawker centre!'

He was especially thrilled to spot a stall that served individual pig parts as he'd also decided to expand his food chart by eating individual parts of species that he'd already consumed. He couldn't get started on this agenda right away because this stall was shut, but expected we'd find something during our numerous hawker centre visits.

Meanwhile, I spotted a juice shop and decided to get some juice. As I read through the menu, I realized there were many new fruits I hadn't heard of like *soursup* and *balonglong*, in addition to the more commonly available fruits like durian, mangoes and dragon fruit. The stall was also advertising the health properties of every juice. Like the herbal remedies at the Imperial, many of these juices were purported to make you look younger by improving the collagen production of the skin. Since I hadn't eaten the goose web or the crocodile tail, I decided I'd aid my pursuit of youth with juice. I decided to try out soursup, a large prickly fruit. It had a strong citrusy-sweet taste, which made it the perfect refreshing drink for the hot afternoon.

Then we headed to the Tiong Bahru Bakery on Tiong Bahru road, one of the oldest areas in Singapore. Today, it is a hipster area, replete with eclectic cafes, independent coffee shops and eccentric trinket stores. The bakery is one of the best French-style bakeries in Singapore. It was packed with multiple groups of people sitting both inside and outside with cups of coffee and baked goods. I tried to sneak looks at the plates to figure out what was popular.

We headed up to the counter and were faced with a dazzling array of decadent pastries to choose from. We ordered the *kougin amman*, a local bread cake with layers of butter and sugar folded in. We also got an almond chocolate croissant and some coffee to wash it all down.

The almond chocolate croissant was light and airy, with a good amount of the chocolate filling and sprinkled almonds.

Kougin amman and other baked delights

The kougin amman was a perfect blend of butter and sugar and was really soft.

Both the pastries were melt-in-the-mouth delicious, so, we made sure to pack some apple pie and a chocolate croissant to take home with us for Amita and the twins. Singapore was turning out to be a food paradise. Like everything else in the city, their food was also perfect.

Tiong Bahru Bakery, Tiong Bahru Road		
Item	*Kougin Amman*	*Almond Chocolate Croissant*
Taste	★★★★★	★★★★★
Price	SGD8	SGD4
Fear Factor	1	1
New Species	None	None

Journey to the Hawker Centre of the Earth

A bulk of our trip was spent visiting numerous hawker centres, allowing us to consume multiple meals a day. It helped that we took the bus, which meant that all the walking increased our appetites. Our first big meal at a hawker centre was on our second day in Singapore, after an 8-km cycle ride through the East Coast Park, the country's largest seafront park.

The East Coast Park is built on reclaimed land with a manmade beach nearby, making it a very popular weekend destination. Our motley crew of riders included Anupam, Amita and their twins. Along the way, we spotted many barbecue pits and camping areas where people were setting up picnic lunches and tents. At the many piers, people were setting up fishing lines. Vivek was quite disappointed he didn't bring his fishing rod for the trip, never mind the fact that the rod has been in its packaging for over five years! We rode alongside the sea, with the ocean breeze whipping through our hair and cooling us down. We rode until we hit the East Coast Lagoon Food Village and found a table near the sea and the children's play area.

East Coast Lagoon Food Village is one of the larger food centres in the country. The enclosed area that houses the food stalls is a few metres away from the picnic tables by the beach.

It also had seating areas on the periphery, as well as at the centre. As always, Vivek and I first took a walk around the entire enclosure so we could scope out all the food available before we made our choice.

Vivek was eager to try out other parts of pork and was trying to locate a stall similar to the one he had spotted at the Zion food centre the previous evening. Surprisingly, there was no such stall in sight. In fact, most of the stalls proudly advertised 'No Pork, No Lard'. Anupam, who was walking with us, while Amita and the twins held our table, suspected that this park was adjacent to a housing union that catered to the local Muslim population and therefore did not serve pork. The closeness to the sea meant that there was a wide variety of seafood, including stingray, crabs, clams, crayfish and more.

We examined the menus at every stall and Vivek also looked at the creatures on display in the aquariums. Suddenly, we spotted crayfish. Or rather, what the Singaporeans were calling crayfish. Vivek was quite certain it wasn't crayfish. He said this was a Moreton Bay bug, something he missed eating in Australia and had been hunting for ever since. Either way, we decided to get it. If it was a Moreton Bay bug, he would have a new species. If not, it would be a new experience. We requested the owner to show us the 'crayfish' so Vivek could pick his favourite and take a photo so as to verify the species later. The owner showed us three of them in a plastic basket. Vivek turned them over to examine them from all angles. One of them still had the egg sac, which meant he would get two for the price of one—the crustacean and the roe! He asked for it to be cooked. Anupam decided to head to another stall while we waited for the 'crayfish'.

We also ordered a plate of cockles. A cockle is a small, bivalve mollusc. They look like the shells you find on the beach and can be opened up and eaten in the manner of oysters. Cockles are found in sandy, sheltered beaches throughout the world. We sat down by the stall while our 'crayfish' and cockles were getting ready. I took a walk to a juice stall nearby and got some sugar cane juice, the Singaporean staple, to beat the heat. When I got back, Vivek told me he was also going to get a Century Egg. Typically, Century Eggs are added to other dishes for flavour, however, Vivek was able to get a plate of the eggs to taste them by themselves. He knew that they were technically rotten, but wanted to break through the mental barrier.

We collected our order and headed to our table by the sea. We met Anupam as we were exiting the food centre. He had purchased *popiah* from Eastern Red Seafood, carrot cake from Lagoon Carrot Cake and *char kway teo* from Choon Hiang, all of which are the top-rated dishes at East Coast Lagoon. Our table was soon filled with trays of food.

We started with the popiah, a Fujianese-style spring roll. The wheat flour skin is crepe-like, soft and viscous. It's filled with grated, steamed turnip, bean sprouts, jicama, lettuce leaves, carrots, tofu, chopped peanuts, shallots, Chinese sausage and shredded omelette. It's soft, with a crunchy filling.

We then moved on to the carrot cake, which is neither made of carrots nor is it a cake. Instead, it's a savoury dish made of rice flour and white radish, also called white carrot, which gives the dish its name. This mixture is steamed, cut into cubes and fried with garlic, eggs and served with a kind of preserved radish called *chai poh*. It is served in two versions— black, fried with dark soya sauce, or white, the original. We had a mix of both. The black was more flavourful, as it had a sweet taste from the soya sauce that complimented the savoury taste of the dish.

Beginning our feast with char kway teo

The best of the three non-seafood dishes was the char kway teo, or 'stir-fried rice cake strips', a Malaysian noodle dish. A dish originally sold by fishermen, farmers and cockle gatherers, its origins are from frying any leftover fish or meat with pork lard and rice noodles to sell to workers and supplement their income. The wok frying gives the dish its characteristic slightly sweet, charred taste.

The supposed crayfish was Vivek's favourite.

As he began digging into the crustacean, he said, 'The best thing about large crustaceans is that once you remove the hard skin shell, there is a large amount of juicy meat just waiting for you inside. There are no bones, no scales and no cartilage—nothing to get in your way. In my opinion, crustaceans are the fruit of the sea. All you need to do is peel them and enjoy the fruit!'

Amita and Anupam looked bemused. While they all enjoyed both the meat and the roe, Vivek continued to look troubled by the fact that this was called a 'crayfish'. However, we didn't have Internet access at the time so he needed to wait until we got home to find out what he was eating.

The cockles were also a hit, though we had such a large portion that it took a while for them to get through the entire plate. They came with skewers and chopsticks to pry open the shell and get to the meat inside, as well as some lemon and chilli sauce to add flavour.

Cockles

We sat at the table for over an hour as we got through the large amount of food we'd ordered. It worked well for the twins as they were able to build sandcastles for a long time without anyone asking them to leave. One of them even managed to find an abandoned toy car that they appropriated, so Vivek wasn't the only one who found something new.

Later that day, Vivek finally determined that he had indeed managed to find Moreton Bay bugs. He was thrilled he'd been proven right and that the entire hawker centre was mistaken. The crustacean he'd eaten that day had a flat head, characteristic to a Moreton Bay bug. It also had claws that weren't extended in the manner of the crayfish he'd eaten in Vietnam, further confirming the species.

East Coast Lagoon Food Centre, 1220 East Coast Park						
Item	Cockles	Moreton Bay Bugs	Popiah	Carrot Cake	Char Kwey Teo	Century Eggs
Taste	★★★	★★★★	★★★★	★★★	★★★★★	★★★★
Price	SGD4	SGD6	SGD3	SGD3	SGD5	SGD1
Fear Factor	3	3	2	2	2	5
New Species	Cockles	Moreton Bay Bug	None	None	None	Fermented Eggs

~

Our next stop was the Newton Food Centre, a food centre highly recommended as one of the best places to try out the local specialties—chilli crab and pepper crab. We wandered around to see if the market had anything else to offer before we zeroed in on the crab. While many stalls were advertising crab, very few had a display. Since Vivek was particular about being able to pick out his crab, we stopped at Heng Heng Barbeque. They had a display set out in the front of the stall and were able to show him a few options. Once he picked out his crab, it was cooked fresh as we waited.

Jumbo pepper crab

Eating crabs is a very messy process as one needs to break open the shell and pick through the meat. Vivek got to work and pronounced the crab worth all the effort and the mess. Every bite of the soft crabmeat was infused with a sweet pepper sauce. It was perfectly flavoured, with the kick of pepper evening out the sweetness and tang in the sauce. We spent the better part of an hour there, as Vivek cracked open the crab and made sure he got into every crevice and savoured every bite.

Heng Heng Barbecue, 500 Clemencau Avenue North, Newton Centre	
Item	*Pepper Crab*
Taste	★★★★★
Price	SGD40
Fear Factor	2
New Species	None

~

Afterwards, I decided to stop by one of the stalls selling dessert to get the ice *kachang*, a local dessert of Malay origin made of shaved ice, multicoloured syrup and topped with red beans, sweet corn and agar. Popular toppings include sweet corn, peanuts, evaporated or condensed milk, mangoes, durian, ice cream, basil syrup or *chendol*.* We decided to get the one with durian.

It looked like a towering mound of rainbow coloured ice *gola*. As a gola lover, I was expecting to like this. Unfortunately, it was overwhelmingly sweet. I didn't like the sweet red bean corn syrup mix. I did, however, like the durian, so I isolated it and had it with some shaved ice that hadn't yet absorbed the sickeningly sweet taste of the other toppings.

Thankfully, the ice kachang was not the only Singaporean sweet dish I tried. I also ate copious amounts of kaya toast, the local breakfast sandwich. Kaya is a local coconut jam. Kaya toast is basically toast and butter, with a layer of kaya added to it. The salt in the butter cuts through the sweetness of the kaya to make a great toast. I first got kaya toast at the Toast Box, a local franchise that's all around Singapore.

It was one of those comfort staples I could get while Vivek looked for his next species.

Newton Food Centre, Newton	
Item	*Durian Ice Kachang*
Taste	★
Price	SGD2
Fear Factor	2
New Species	None

~

* Rice flour jelly

On our third day, we went to the Old Airport Road food centre for brunch. I stopped at the first bakery we found to buy cheese bread, chicken curry bread and fish puffs. I was already a fan of baked goods in Singapore, after Tiong Bahru Bakery and the kaya toast, and the cheese bread did not disappoint. It was actually a bun with a cheese filling as well as cheese baked on the top. The fish puffs looked like *gujiyas* and came with a spicy fish filling.

Old Airport Road Food Centre turned out to be crucial for Vivek as he was finally able to find a place that sold pork. At Shop No 01–106, Old Airport Road Mixed Pork Soup, they were selling organ soup, which topped the list of weird things he'd eaten. Typically, organs are thrown away and only the meat and limbs of animals are cooked. However, like many other parts of Southeast Asia, Singapore also uses up organs in food. It was a huge mental barrier for Vivek to overcome as he had to try out a soup that was made entirely out of what are essentially 'reject' parts. He wanted to try this because he felt that the use of organs justified the butchery of the animal. Why waste parts once the animal had been sacrificed for food?

Organ soup tasted very different from one that would use flesh. The liver was coarse, intestines chewy—neither of these textures felt like meat. Since Vivek was in the mode of attempting a new experience, he almost found it tasty. In fact, he said he could get used to this if he had to.

Meanwhile, I spotted a huge line outside Xin Mei Xing Lor Mee, so I joined it to see what the fuss was about. Lor Mee is a Chinese inspired noodle dish. Unlike most noodle dishes that have a soupy broth base, this one has a thick, starchy gravy. The gravy is made of corn starch, spices and eggs. The stall offered a choice between flat noodles and rice noodles with toppings like fish, pork and egg. It was quite clear why it was so popular. The broth was tangy, with a little bit of a sweet aftertaste. It was sublime and most definitely the best thing I ate in Singapore.

Pigs' organ soup: Boundaries are in our minds

Old Airport Road Food Centre, 51 Old Airport Road		
Item	*Egg Lor Mee*	*Organ Soup*
Taste	★★★★★	★★★
Price	SGD4	SGD3.5
Fear Factor	2	5
New Species	None	Parts: Stomach, Kidney, Intestine

~

From the food centre, we headed to Gardens by the Bay where the Flower Dome had a Sakura festival going on. After a couple of hours spent at the Dome, we headed out to the Upper

Book Keng Market and Food Centre because Vivek's research indicated that there was goat tongue soup there. We didn't get our hopes up because we have often been disappointed to discover that a certain dish is no longer available. But, this was one of those times when we were in luck and Vivek got his soup.

Goat's tongue soup

I had heard that tongues have a distinct texture and taste,' he said. 'Now I can see why that's the case. The tongue has so many strong muscles and no bones, so it has a unique texture!' The tongue is cooked for several hours to ensure that it's tender enough to eat. Every piece of it felt like a dense block of meat. On the surface, you could feel the texture of the tongue which had absorbed the flavours of the soup and was both spicy and salty. The meaty parts were like the most premium cuts of lamb sliced by the most skilful butcher and cooked by the best chef in the world.

Between the organ soup and the tongue soup, day three turned out to be a good day for Vivek's new resolution to branch out into body parts. The attempt also helped him break through a mental barrier of eating parts that are typically not eaten, at least in India.

Haji M Abdul Rajak Stall, Upper Boon Keng Market and Food Centre	
Item	*Tongue Soup*
Taste	★★★★★
Price	SGD6
Fear Factor	5
New Species	None

~

Earlier that day, a cab driver had mentioned that the best durians in Singapore could be found at the fruit shops on Sims Road. We were very close to Sims Road and Vivek wanted to take a walk to work off some of his double lunch. He also finally wanted to eat durian. Since we had already experimented with durian juice and the durian on the ice kachang, we decided it was time for us to get over our fear of the smell. We were able to locate the stall fairly easily and bought cut pieces of durian. It was the tourists' way of trying out the fruit because all around us we could see the locals cutting it themselves. We spotted signs talking about the public transport ban on durian earlier that day on the bus.[37] I definitely did not want to cut a durian as I was concerned about the smell sticking to my fingers. I was nervous about even eating the cut fruit, but I steeled myself mentally with the thought that Vivek had eaten many bizarre things so I had to try a fruit, at least!

I decided to take the plunge quite literally and had a big bite. Cut durian didn't just look like jackfruit, it also tasted a lot like jackfruit. Since people in Southeast Asia refer to it as the king of fruits, I assumed it would be sweet. Instead, it was a new and interesting mix of sweet and savoury with a creamy texture. It was quite easy to eat the fruit, but it definitely wasn't my favourite. I think I'll stick to the Indian definition of the king of fruits, mango. Vivek, however, is always pleased when he conquers his food fears so he insisted that durian was superior to mango. I let him praise it so I could later claim all the mangoes back home and send him on a wild goose chase for durian!

~

We saved the best for the last day when we headed out to the popular Maxwell Food Centre. Home to the famous Tian Tian Chicken Rice praised by Anthony Bourdain,[38] this food centre is packed at lunchtime. The chicken rice proved itself very worthy of the praise.

The rice was fluffy and so well cooked that you could've eaten it as a dish on its own and not felt like you missed out! The chicken was braised and came with a spicy sauce.

While Vivek ate the famous Michelin-starred chicken rice, I had kaya toast and tried out a new juice—this time balonglong, also known as *kedongdeong* in Malaysia. The stall advertised it as rich in antioxidants and good for digestion. My taste buds were fired up by this juice, which was bright green and had a rich chlorophyll like aftertaste. It was so refreshing I forgot that I was in a crowded, humid food centre on a hot day.

The famous Tian Tian Chicken Rice

Through our visits to the hawker centres, we were able to truly experience the diversity of cultures in Singapore. We found foods from around the world and they were still the cheapest meals we had. I was especially proud of the fact that I'd finally managed an eating expedition of my own by eating durian for the very first time.

Tian Tian, #1 10/11 Maxwell Food Centre, 1 Kadayanallur Street	
Item	*Chicken Rice*
Taste	★★★
Price	SGD5
Fear Factor	1
New Species	None

Dead Men Tell No Tastes

One of the biggest reasons for an adventurous foodie to visit Japan is fugu or puffer fish. Whoever ate the first puffer fish was definitely an adventurist and probably died soon after. Puffer fish, also called blowfish, contain a highly toxic poison in its organs called tetrodotoxin. Despite this, fugu has been eaten in Japan for hundreds of years. Initially, it was unknown how to properly prepare the fish, resulting in many fatalities, resulting in a ban on the fish between 1570 to 1870.[39] Nowadays, fugu is available in Japan but is prohibited from being cooked at home. It can only be prepared by a licensed chef, for which the training process takes at least two years and one-third of the trainees do not qualify. Licensed chefs will remove the toxin-ridden organs and then tip them into a metal drum locked with a padlock. The parts are taken to a fish market and burned.

Accidentally eating a toxic piece of fugu leads to a particularly awful death—first your lips start tingling and soon numbness spreads through your body. Eventually, you die through suffocation, remaining conscious throughout the process. This is one of the reasons why it almost always tops the list of the worlds' most bizarre foods.

Fugu was always on top of Vivek's list of things to eat for when we eventually go to Japan. This was before he discovered that Guenpin Fugu, Japan's top tora-fugu restaurant had opened their first overseas branch in Singapore. Tora-fugu, or tiger puffer fish, is renowned as the highest grade of puffer fish. Most of the fugu at Guenpin is flown in from Shimonoseki, Japan's puffer fish capital. Vivek booked a reservation for lunch on our last day, which also happened to be a day before his thirty-fifth birthday. He is typically courageous when it comes to food, but he went back and forth on this plan many times. While the stats vary, in spite of all the protective methods, there are still a few people who die of fugu poisoning every year. While he steeled himself towards this experiment, I spent most of our trip wondering if he'd survive to see his birthday or if this quest had finally gone a step too far.

Guenpin Fugu is easy to find—it's easily accessible from Exit B of Tanjong Pagar MRT station. The restaurant is tucked away in Maxwell Chambers. It has an elaborate fugu and snow crab menu. Vivek was keen on trying the sushi and sashimi because they would give him the best opportunity to taste the fish.

The sashimi was thinly sliced and translucent. It was laid out in the shape of a chrysanthemum, which is a tongue-in-cheek prophetic touch as chrysanthemum is the flower symbolizing death in Japan.

The sashimi was served with radish, spring onions and a ponzu soy sauce. Vivek got to work topping up the sashimi with the veggies and dipping it into the soy sauce. Puffer fish has a rubbery texture and a very mild taste. The radish, spring onions and sauce bring out the flavours in the dish.

The sushi was very well made, but again, the taste of the puffer fish is really mild. Vivek was very glad that he'd tried it raw and could get the full extent of the taste even if it was mild compared to some other fish. He really liked it. Fugu is a dish where he can remember every bit of the taste, given that his senses were on super alert while he ate it. After all, it was a matter of life and death!

Fugu sushi: Dare eat that?

Just as he polished off the sushi and I was mentally thanking our stars that he survived, he began coughing. His eyes were watering.

'I feel weird,' he choked out as he clutched at his throat.

My mind went into overdrive as I began wondering if this was the first sign of fugu poisoning. Maybe the choking was followed by tingly lips and paralysis? I tried to recall whether our travel insurance would cover voluntary fugu poisoning when I realized that this was a very delayed reaction. He'd spent over twenty minutes eating both the sashimi and the sushi before he'd started squeaking out his words. Also, it was nearly impossible to get poisoned in Singapore because the import laws are so strict that they recheck for toxins along multiple steps before the fugu is let into the country.

My gaze wandered to the side of his plate and suddenly the pieces fell into place.

'You just decided to test your bravery by finishing all the wasabi, didn't you?' I asked with narrowed eyes.

'Well, the fugu didn't provide enough of a thrill. I was hoping for some tingly lips to get my money's worth. Besides, we just spent almost forty Singapore dollars on this meal and I'm not wasting a single thing on my plate,' he wheezed as the sharp taste of the wasabi shot up his nose.

I no longer had any sympathy for his 'weird' feeling.

Guenpin Fugu, Maxwell Chambers, Maxwell Road		
Item	*Torafugu Sashimi*	*Torafugu Sushi*
Taste	★★★★	★★★
Price	SGD8.8	SGD30
Fear Factor	10/5!	10/5!
New Species	Puffer fish	Puffer fish

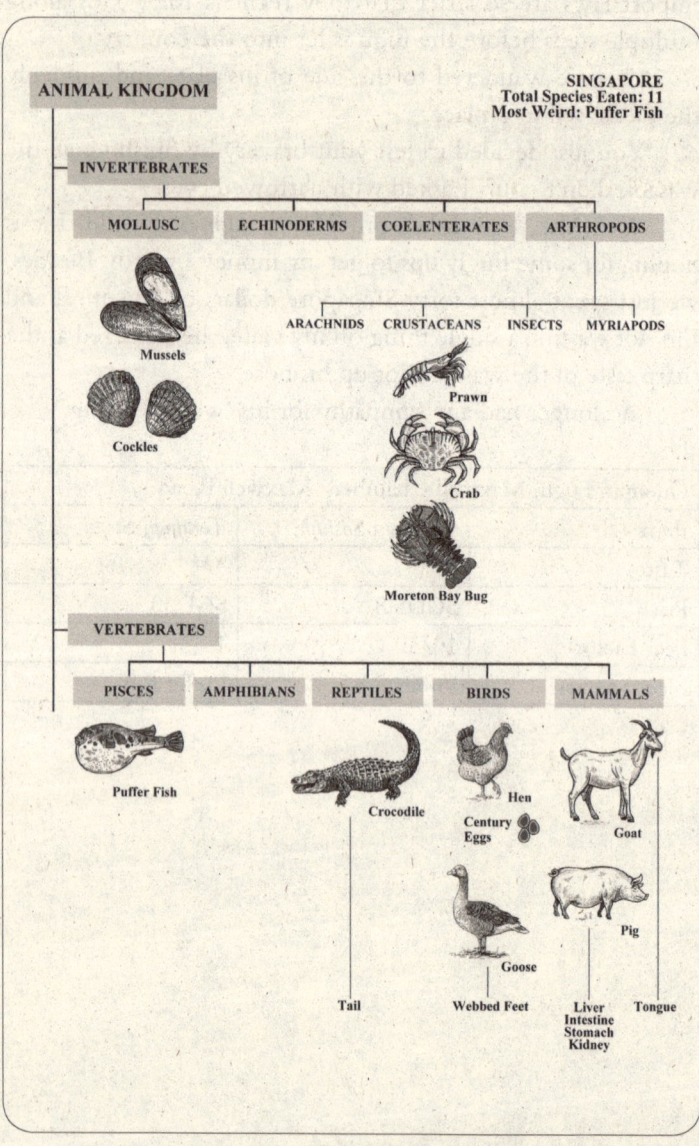

ANIMAL KINGDOM

SINGAPORE
Total Species Eaten: 11
Most Weird: Puffer Fish

INVERTEBRATES

MOLLUSC ECHINODERMS COELENTERATES ARTHROPODS

ARACHNIDS CRUSTACEANS INSECTS MYRIAPODS

Mussels

Cockles

Prawn

Crab

Moreton Bay Bug

VERTEBRATES

PISCES AMPHIBIANS REPTILES BIRDS MAMMALS

Puffer Fish

Crocodile

Hen
Century
Eggs

Goat

Goose

Pig

Tail

Webbed Feet

Liver
Intestine
Stomach
Kidney

Tongue

Afterword

'Look over there! That shop is called Buffalo Café and it's selling Wild Buffalo Soup,' I said, as we walked down a road in Nikko, East Japan.

'Actually, it says Wild Buffalo Shop, not Soup,' Vivek said. 'You've spent too much time with me—you now see bizarre food everywhere!'

Over the past four years, we've travelled around the world in search of the next interesting species for Vivek to eat. Through this process, we've each learned from each other's travel styles—I am now more open to a less planned schedule and more food-centred stops and he has been to more museums, temples and castles than he would've seen otherwise. Our most memorable trips have not been about what we saw, or even, what he ate. It's been about travelling together and the joys of exploring and experiencing it through the eyes of someone who approaches things very differently. Today, I know a lot more about food, why we eat what we eat and the future of food than I'd have ever known otherwise. He, in turn, says that he has seen new worlds and alternate realities, a bigger universe, because of me.

We haven't yet finished travelling all around the world (my goal) or eaten every bizarre species (his goal), but we're well on our way. In this journey, we have had some great adventures like surviving fugu, making our own ant egg bhurji, discovering emus and rabbits in India, finding fried sparrows in Cambodia and more. We are sometimes disappointed when he is thwarted in his attempts to find and eat a particular species, like the still-elusive rats, but Vivek says this is for the best. Our search for the elusive species and other new ones continue on every trip we take, leading us to new, rich experiences.

As I complete this book, we are mid-way through a trip to Japan where we located *shirako* at the Nishiki market in Kyoto. We look forward to finding more bizarre foods like sea cucumber in China, locusts in Africa, sago worms in Malaysian Borneo or Papua New Guinea and lizards in rural Spain. Closer home, we haven't yet crossed that great frontier of Indian food, the North East, so we haven't yet experienced the local grubs from the insect markets of Kohima. We also haven't had the Chhattisgarh specialty of *chaprah* or red ant chutney. Some of these eluded us in countries we've been to—the locusts were not in season when we were in Vietnam. Others are from parts of the world we are still to visit. Others still aren't on the list yet because even Vivek hasn't had the courage to consider them.

And so, there are many specialties that remain on the list and the list continues to grow. There's always something new as we make our way around the world—this journey is more enjoyable than any destination and thus our journey continues.

Acknowledgements

Amma and Appa for always encouraging me to follow my dreams, irrespective of how bizarre some of them sounded. I wouldn't be half the person I am today, without your unflinching support.

My greatest cheerleader, my brother Adithya. Thank you for letting me claim that I was your 'babysitter' when all I did was wave a rattle in your screaming face while I continued to read.

Archana Iyer, for reading every version of this manuscript and giving me your brutally honest feedback every time. I'm sure there were other books you could've read on your long flights, but you chose mine. For that and for everything else, you will always be my person.

Gaurav Tripathi and Richa Tripathi, Shreyas, Anupam Dikhit and Amita Singh—friends who hosted us, for not batting an eyelid when they saw the animal charts. Thank you for accompanying (and sometimes guiding!) us on our out-of-the-ordinary excursions. I promise we didn't secretly cook any bizarre foods in your kitchens.

Mithila Kulkarni for her feedback on the manuscript and for her recommendation that every chapter should include a map.

Foodie Adventurers—Kaushik Mitra, Jayant Mahto, Amit Madke, Dinesh Arora and Piyush May, for enthusiastically participating in the quest. Saurav Patnaik, for impromptu plans involving a road trip, a village, camping and fishing. You checked all of Vivek's boxes in one trip, something I still haven't managed!

Diptakirti Chaudhuri—for believing in me. Thank you for helping me find a home for this book.

Zarreen Khan and Issac John, friends and fellow writers, for patiently and promptly responding to my numerous questions about writing and getting published.

Amit Garg for all his advice and support. Thank you for going above and beyond for me every time.

Anisha Arvind—watching you read keeps me hopeful about the future of reading and writing. I hope that all my readers roll off the bed laughing like you did when you heard your uncle ate a horse.

My grandparents—A.V. Sathyakaman, Uma Sathyakaman, A.K. Srinivasan and Saraswathy Srinivasan for taking inordinate pride in all my achievements. Hopefully, the countless hours spent in ferrying me to the library every other day have finally paid off!

Mummy and Papa for being such inspirations themselves and for their encouragement in all that I do.

Chandhrika Venkataraman, Soumya Sampath, Navia Shetty and Gayathri Arumugam for being my go-to people for random thoughts, rants and everything in between. You help me preserve my sanity.

My family on both sides of the ocean—Sharanya Dilip, Shrikala Kashyap, Aparna Sridhar, Aarti Kashyap and Narayanan Kashyap for their enthusiasm and encouragement. Arvind Sridhar, Sunayana Joshi, Janani Vasudev and Karthik Srinivasan for ensuring that the US will always feel like another home.

My professors—A.B. Kulkarni who always believed I would do something creative, thus pushing me to create. Renuka Kamath for being the sounding board for all my existential questions.

Prof. Marti Hearst, Prof. Kimiko Ryokai and the WordCraft team for co-authoring the paper that took us to London.

Gurveen Chadha at Penguin Random House for relentlessly championing my writing. Thank you for your feedback—every one of your suggestions went a long way towards making this book what it is.

Last but never the least, V for being the first reader and best critic of every thing I write.. Thank you for the adventures that led to this book. I couldn't have asked for a better co-traveller for all of life's journeys.

Notes

1. Rich McEachran, 'Food of the Future: What Will Feed 7 Billion People', *Guardian* (2014).
   https://www.theguardian.com/global-development-professionals-network/2014/aug/12/insects-algae-lab-meat-food
2. Jules Verne, *Around the World in Eighty Days*
3. *Atlas Obscura: Gum Wall*
   https://www.atlasobscura.com/places/gum-wall
4. 'Anyway, like I was sayin', shrimp is the fruit of the sea,' by Bubba in *Forrest Gump*, 1994
5. Southwest Fisheries Science Centre
   https://swfsc.noaa.gov/textblock.aspx?Division=FRD&id=20568
6. Sabyasachi Roy Chaudhuri, 'Patthar ka Ghosht: The Delicacy from the Nizami Era', *New Indian Express*
   http://www.newindianexpress.com/cities/hyderabad/2017/sep/22/patthar-ka-gosht-the-delicacy-from-the-nizami-era-1661267.html
7. Stephen Halliday, 'Underneath the Arches: Celebrating Borough Market', *History Today*
   https://www.historytoday.com/stephen-halliday/underneath-arches-celebrating-borough-market
8. Steve Mbogo, 'Hoteliers Push for Lifting of Game Meat and Import Ban', *Business Daily Africa*

https://www.businessdailyafrica.com/corporate/Hoteliers-push-for-lifting-of-game-meat-sale-and-import-ban/539550-1045586-th20ux/index.html

9. Stephen Moss, '*The Mousetrap* at 60: Why is this the World's Longest Running Play', *Guardian* (2012)
https://www.theguardian.com/stage/2012/nov/20/mousetrap-60-years-agatha-christie

10. Felicity Lawrence, 'Horsemeat Scandal: The Essential Guide', *Guardian* (2013)
https://www.theguardian.com/uk/2013/feb/15/horsemeat-scandal-the-essential-guide

11. R.T. Gahukar, 'Edible Insects Farming: Efficiency and Impact on Family Livelihood, Food Security and Environment Compared with Livestock and Crops', *Insects as Sustainable Food Ingredients—Science Direct*
https://www.sciencedirect.com/topics/agricultural-and-biological-sciences/weaver-ant

12. Alice Shen, 'Boat Noodles: The Secrets to Thai Dish's Great Taste and Five Places to Eat Them in Hong Kong', *SCMP*
https://www.scmp.com/lifestyle/food-drink/article/2114920/boat-noodles-secrets-thai-dishs-great-taste-and-five-places-eat

13. 'Wat Arun in Bangkok—Temple of Dawn', *Bangkok.com*
http://www.bangkok.com/attraction-temple/wat-arun.htm

14. Erik Trinidad, 'Waiter, There's Spit in My Soup: A Review', *Cooking Channel TV* (2013)
https://www.cookingchanneltv.com/devour/2013/05/what-is-birds-nest-soup

15. Kelly Iverson, 'An Introduction to Thailand's Floating Markets', *Culture Trip*
https://theculturetrip.com/asia/thailand/articles/an-introduction-to-thailands-floating-markets/

16. Macquarie Lighthouse
https://www.sydney.com/destinations/sydney/sydney-east/attractions/macquarie-lighthouse

17. Sydney Fish Market: Our Company
    https://www.sydneyfishmarket.com.au/our-company/our-company

18. Graham Lloyd, 'The Oldest Rainforest', *Australian*, (2011)
    https://www.theaustralian.com.au/life/weekend-australian-magazine/the-oldest-rainforest/news-story/c336bc382a428c33adfe16d8a344e2a3

19. 'Angkor Wat', *History.com*
    https://www.history.com/topics/landmarks/angkor-wat

20. Anil Gurung, 'Cuisine Spawned by the Khmer Rouge: Must-try Local Delicacies in Siem Reap Today', *The Backstreet Academy Blog* (2015)
    https://www.backstreetacademy.com/blog/cuisine-spawned-by-the-khmer-rouge-must-try-local-delicacies-in-siem-reap-today/

21. Marissa, 'Ta Phrom: Cambodia's Tomb Raider Temple', *The Culture Trip* (2018)
    https://theculturetrip.com/asia/cambodia/articles/ta-prohm-cambodias-tomb-raider-temple/

22. Rich McEachran, 'Are Seaweed Snacks the Future as Tide Turns on Meat Consumption', *Guardian* (2014)
    https://www.theguardian.com/sustainable-business/2014/nov/05/seaweed-burgers-snack-meat-consumption-resources

23. 'Kompong Khleang Travel', *Lonely Planet*
    https://www.lonelyplanet.com/cambodia/kompong-khleang

24. Joseph Freeman, 'In Phnom Penh, Cambodia the French Influence Lives On', *Washington Post* (2014)
    https://www.washingtonpost.com/lifestyle/travel/in-phnom-penh-cambodia-the-french-influence-lives-on/2014/01/23/8023ea12-7eec-11e3-9556-4a4bf7bcbd84_story.html?noredirect=on&utm_term=.89a1fd43299f

25. 'Notre Dame Cathedral', *Lonely Planet*
    https://www.lonelyplanet.com/vietnam/ho-chi-minh-city/attractions/notre-dame-cathedral/a/poi-sig/403218/357884

26. 'Saigon Central Post Office—Ho Chi Minh City', *Atlas Obscura* https://www.atlasobscura.com/places/saigon-central-post-office

27. Dung Phan, 'The Cu Chi Tunnels Are a Must Visit to Remember Vietnam's Underground War', *The Culture Trip* (2017) https://theculturetrip.com/asia/vietnam/articles/the-cu-chi-tunnels-are-a-must-visit-to-remember-vietnams-underground-war/

28. 'Mekong Delta', *Lonely Planet* https://www.lonelyplanet.com/vietnam/mekong-delta

29. 'Weasel Coffee: You're Going to Drink What', *The Smithsonian* (2011) https://www.smithsonianmag.com/arts-culture/weasel-coffee-youre-going-to-drink-what-26514211/

30. 'Discover Phu Quoc National Park in Vietnam', *Phu Quoc Island Guide* https://www.phuquocislandguide.com/phu-quoc-national-park/

31. Lewis Carroll, *Alice's Adventures in Wonderland and Through the Looking Glass*, Penguin, reissue edition, 2003

32. 'One Pillar Pagoda', *Lonely Planet* https://www.lonelyplanet.com/vietnam/hanoi/attractions/one-pillar-pagoda/a/poi-sig/1141850/357880

33. Katie Kalmusky, 'A Guide to Hanoi's Temple of Literature', *The Culture Trip* (2018) https://theculturetrip.com/asia/vietnam/articles/a-guide-to-hanois-temple-of-literature/

34. 'Vietnamese Prison: Hanoi Hilton', *Learning History* https://www.learning-history.com/vietnamese-prison-hanoi-hilton/

35. Rob Crilly, 'Barack Obama Treated to $6 Noodles by Anthony Bourdain in Hanoi', *Telegraph* (2016) https://www.telegraph.co.uk/news/2016/05/23/barack-obama-treated-to-6-noodles-in-hanoi-by-anthony-bourdain/

36. Lauren Jade Hill, 'Anthony Bourdain: My First Trip to Vietnam Changed My Life', *Conde Nast Traveller* (2014)
https://www.cntraveller.com/stories/2014-09-26/anthony-bourdain-my-first-trip-to-vietnam-changed-my-life

37. Joseph Stromberg, 'Why Does the Durian Fruit Smell So Terrible', *The Smithsonian* (2012)
https://www.smithsonianmag.com/science-nature/why-does-the-durian-fruit-smell-so-terrible-149205532/

38. David Farley, 'The Dish Worth a 15 Hour Flight', *BBC Travel* (2015)
http://www.bbc.com/travel/story/20151105-the-singapore-dish-worth-a-15-hour-flight

39. Danielle Demetriou, 'Tokyo to Relax Rules on Serving Deadly "Fugu" Pufferfish', *Telegraph* (2012)
https://www.telegraph.co.uk/news/worldnews/asia/japan/9125115/Tokyo-to-relax-rules-on-serving-deadly-fugu-puffer-fish.html

Note on the Author

Divya is a product manager who writes six-pagers by day and is an author by night. She gets her best creative ideas when she's hanging upside down at her anti-gravity yoga class or doodling. Her wanderlust gene is a result of having lived in three countries and eight cities. In 2017, she won the Juggernaut Times LitFest Contest for her short story 'That Girl Is Trouble'. Divya has an MBA in Marketing from SPJIMR, Mumbai and a master's in HCI from UC Berkeley, California. When she's not wandering through the food streets of the world, she can be found at home in Bangalore with her husband Vivek. *Dare Eat That* is her first book.

For more photos, videos and travel stories, log onto: www.dareeatthat.com.